skinny-licious

Shauna Evans, RN

skinny-licious

Lite and Scrumptious Recipes for a SLIMMER YOU

Front Table Books
An Imprint of Cedar Fort, Inc.
Springville, Utah

ISBN 13: 978-1-4621-1324-8

Published by Front Table Books, an imprint of Cedar Fort, Inc.
2373 W. 700 S., Springville, UT 84663
Distributed by Cedar Fort, Inc., www.cedarfort.com

Library of Congress Cataloging-in-Publication Data on file

Cover and page design by Erica Dixon
Cover design © 2014 by Lyle Mortimer
Edited by Casey J. Winters

Printed in China

10 9 8 7 6 5 4 3 2 1

To my hunky husband, Joe Evans, for loving me fat, fit, or thin

contents

Acknowledgments ‹‹‹‹‹‹‹‹‹‹‹‹‹‹‹‹

First, I would like to extend my gratitude to David Zinczenko from the bottom of my healthy heart for writing his book, *The 8-Hour Diet*, and sharing the groundbreaking science behind this plan. It changed my life for the better. After years of trying, not only am I slim again, I have a new lease on life, and I have zest.

A shout-out to my former publicist, Chloe Curtis, for prodding me to write this manuscript and share the valuable information and delicious recipes that helped me achieve my weight-loss goals.

This beautiful book would not be the visual treat it is if it were not for the creative talents of its designer, Erica Dixon. I would like to express sincere appreciation to Joanna Barker and Casey Winters for their excellent editing skills and attention to detail. And thanks to Matice McClellan for her marketing help.

Last, I would like to thank the entire staff at Cedar Fort Publishing & Media for their professional work and mission to make a positive difference in the publishing world.

Preface ‹‹‹‹‹‹‹‹‹‹‹‹‹‹‹‹‹‹‹‹‹‹‹‹‹‹‹‹

This book is about my journey going from fit to fat to thin and the method and family-friendly recipes I used to achieve weight-loss success in six months. After some serious health challenges—which included chronic pain, anaphylactic shock, and a handful of weight-promoting, anti-inflammatory drugs used to reverse three serious allergic reactions—I found myself forty-five pounds heavier and still gaining. For the last five years, I struggled to find a weight-loss solution that worked and that I could follow for the remainder of my life. In September 2012, I happened upon a diet regiment by accident. After losing twenty pounds in four weeks, I knew I was on to something spectacular.

In the next few pages, not only will I touch on the difficult weight-loss dilemma I faced, but I will also share some of the groundbreaking and surprising science behind this diet. I lost thirty-five pounds before I discovered that what I had devised for successful weight loss was an actual prescribed plan, called *The 8-Hour Diet* by David Zinczenko. All credit to him in gathering the evidence, studies, facts, and figures and bringing it to the masses in book form in 2012. I wholeheartedly endorse all his tips, suggestions, and eating and exercise advice.

In addition to explaining what it took to take off the weight, I have compiled and created one hundred slimming recipes. The recipes are simple, quick, easy, and delicious—if it doesn't taste good, I don't eat it. This has been my mantra most of my life.

Eating the right foods for weight loss and good health is essential, but so is satisfying our palates. The good news is, I have done a lot of the work for you. With a bachelor's degree in nursing, I have an understanding of diet and fitness principles including what it takes to achieve optimal health through nutrition and exercise. I want you to have the tools and basic knowledge to achieve your own weight-loss success just as I, my husband, sister-in-law, daughter, son, and others did in a few short months. This diet has significantly changed my life for the better, and I want to jump for joy! Join me today in creating the lean, healthy body that you desire by following this prescribed plan and making scrumptious easy-to-prepare foods that will whittle down your waist and trim your thighs.

My Story «««««««««««««««««««««««««

Fortunately, on December 5, 2006, the epinephrine, prednisone, and other anti-inflammatory medications employed to reverse my severe body swelling and life-threatening anaphylaxis was effective in saving my life. Unfortunately, after surviving an emergency allergic reaction, I was faced with a new and surprising challenge—weight gain and an altered, slower metabolism without any lifestyle changes on my part. I exercised and ate as I did before, but I could *not* keep from tipping the scales. Life dealt me a double blow: not only did I reach the age of thirty-five—when women's metabolism and hormones change, making weight control more difficult—but I was also dealing with the negative side effects of prednisone, including a higher set point, sluggish metabolism, and extra pounds.

At the onset of my weight-loss journey, I felt defeated and frustrated. Life gave me a hand that was incredibly unfair. It was not my fault. The first fifteen pounds was largely due to circumstances, and I did nothing of my own accord to deserve it. I did not stuff my face full of cookies and cakes. I still exercised six days a week, but the weight would not budge. I knew it was not my lifestyle or bad habits that got me to this pathetic point.

For the first half of my life, much of my identity was based on my athletic ability and trim, young figure. I was a junior varsity and varsity cheerleader and gymnast at two different high schools. In my teens and twenties, I had completed three marathons. As time progressed, I graduated from Brigham Young University in 1994 with a bachelor's degree in nursing. Even with the stress and pressure of clinical work in hospitals, papers to write, labs to attend, and tests to study for, I remained a size six.

So how in the world could I be sixty pounds overweight *now*? For Pete's sake, I was a woman who knew how to lose extra pounds; my library is full of a dozen diet books and a tall stack of weight-loss and exercise articles. If you asked, I could rattle off the top antioxidants and omega-3 foods. I know my vitamins, minerals, phytochemicals, lycopenes, and correct portion sizes. If you wanted to know, I could accurately categorize a long list of good and bad proteins, carbohydrates, and fats. Some people are walking dictionaries. I am a human calorie counter. Family and friends still come to me to ask how many calories are in the foods they eat, including restaurant fare, and I am

2

incredibly accurate. (It's a lot of fun. You should try it.) So why was I fat? I knew how to lose weight—or so I thought.

For years, I desperately wanted to shed the pounds. I racked my brain with ways to jump-start the process. Pathetically, I started ordering weight-loss supplements online. I purchased Sensa, hoodia, acai berry, and Jillian Michaels's detox kit—all promising rapid weight loss. I was familiar with most diet plans: South Beach, Mediterranean, diabetic exchange, LA weight loss, Atkins, hCG, Paleo, Weight Watchers, glycemic index, Wheat Belly, Nutrisystem, and so on. I tried a variation of some of these and would lose a few measly pounds, but I inevitably gained them back in a short time frame.

Needless to say, none of those weight-loss supplements or schemes worked. I was still steadily gaining. It was like a cruel joke my body and providence were playing on me.

When supplements did not prove effective, I tried to fight it off. In 2010, I joined a gym and began to exercise at least one to two hours a day. I swam, biked, and used the elliptical machine. In August of that year, I signed up and completed the Tri Utah Sprint Triathlon in Orem, Utah. I lost seven pounds but gained them back and maintained my heavy weight for the next two years of my gym membership even with consistently swimming an hour a day five to six days a week. In July 2012, I trained and

successfully completed the Run through the Lavender Half Marathon in Mona, Utah. I had a decent time and lost ten pounds. Six weeks later, I gained the ten back plus twenty more pounds. I was the heaviest weight I had been in my entire life. I would tease that I was fit and fat. But actually I was mad and miserable.

As a registered nurse, I was taught that exercise would increase my metabolism, make it more efficient. Unfortunately, that was not my experience. I was truly frustrated and felt clueless as to how to lose the pounds and keep them off. I felt like I had left no weight-loss stone unturned.

Not only was I fat, wearing a size-fourteen pant, but I was also faced with serious health concerns. My cholesterol level was 247—higher than my mother's, and she was even heavier and shorter than I was. I was at risk for cardiovascular disease. My maternal great-grandmother had a stroke in her 80s and died from the effects of it within a year. My maternal great-aunt died instantly in her early 60s from what we believe was a blood clot. My paternal aunt has type 2 diabetes. In my 41 years, I have had multiple superficial blood clots, lymphedema (swelling) in my legs, and Raynaud's disease. I live in chronic pain and have had multiple vascular procedures or surgeries—fifteen total. And things were not looking up with my high body mass index. In all actuality, I was adding insult to injury since the extra pounds made my health problems worse.

In August 2012, I saw my all-time highest weight, and it almost stopped my heart. I weighed more than I did in my heaviest pregnancy. I was stunned. After years of being consistently overweight, I could no longer wear my beautiful wedding ring and bands, and the mystery still remained. Why was I fat and growing larger? I was stuck. Stuck in a body that did *not* belong to *me*! This was a fat chick's body–not mine. I was stuck with the notion that it was my middle age, hormones, metabolism, and bad luck that kept me fat.

Most people know how to lose weight. But knowing and doing are quite different animals. It all boils down to a sage line by Yoda from *The Empire Strikes Back*: "Do or do not. There is no try."

It was not until I happened upon intermittent fasting that I was able to lose weight successfully and consistently. In September 2012, I had a hard time eating on gameday for my son, who was varsity quarterback. I was too nervous for him to swallow, chew, and digest. After four Friday night games, I noticed something remarkable in my weight: I had lost twenty pounds. I could not believe my eyes—I had struggled with losing more than ten pounds at a time. With this wonderful surprise, I tried to figure out what I had done differently during the past month that I had not done before. The answer: I participated in "accidental" mini fasts.

Mulling over this "new" information in my mind, I recalled a time in 2010 when I did a spiritual fast once a week. I would go without food and water for close to twenty-four hours. I lost twelve pounds doing this for about six consecutive weeks, but I realized that I could not adhere to this plan for the rest of my life; it was too miserable. So I abandoned ship, and the weight came flooding back. However, the principle of the diet still lingered in my mind.

What I Did to Lose Weight and Why It Worked

‹‹‹‹‹‹‹‹‹‹‹‹‹

I decided upon a fasting variation to lose weight—I would stop eating between six and eight o'clock at night, and I would skip breakfast. This is what I dubbed a "mini fast." At the time, I had no knowledge that this was already an "actual" diet. Doing the calculations without much math work, I realized that going without food for that amount of time would inevitably bring my calories down. Skipping breakfast did not break my heart because I wasn't a big breakfast fan in the first place. I determined to begin eating each day when I was close to famished. It became a challenge to see how long I could go before I ate my first meal. My average fast-breaking time is twelve o'clock. Fortunately, I am not ravenous in the early morning hours. The next month of mini fasting resulted in a ten-pound weight loss. The scale was evidence that I was on to something. I was down thirty pounds in two months. I did a little victory dance. No one noticed with the first ten pounds. With twenty pounds, my family began to notice. With thirty pounds, other people started to notice.

After I lost the first thirty pounds, I got a call from my mom. She said that there was a new diet called "the 8-hour diet" by David Zinczenko, which resembles my personally designed diet plan almost identically. Mr. Zinczenko had just been on *Today* discussing this incredible diet and the breakthrough science behind it. Needless to say, I was intrigued. As I read his book, *The 8-Hour Diet*, I grinned through every page. First, the pressure was off because I had lost thirty-five pounds and was no longer overweight. Second, the motivation to go forward and keep up my healthy new habits was reinforced with the overwhelming and welcome science that substantiated the method I used to lose the weight that so easily beset me and clung to me for five fettered years!

This is what scientists have recently discovered: we are asking the wrong question. Weight gain is not as connected to what we eat as it is to *when* we eat. Dr. Satchidananda Panda of the Salk Institute found that with our increased ability to control light via electricity in the last seventy-five years, our eating patterns are abnormally skewed from what they were when our ancestors rose and retired with the sun. Many of us tend to mindlessly eat from morning until midnight. Not only do we start early, often with a sugar- or fat-laden breakfast, but we also keep eating into the twilight hours, making refrigerator raids before bed.[1]

In essence, I subscribed to the 8:16 eating-to-fasting ratio that David Zinczenko suggests. In his book, the following analogy is used: Our body is like an office building open from nine to five. Ideally, we put in eight hours of work, and then we close up shop, go home, and relax. While we are at home with our pajamas on, feet up, and reclining on the couch, the cleaning crew arrives at the office building where we had put in all that hard work. They are there to wipe up spills, take out the trash, and clean the bathrooms. (You get the picture.) Our body's cells or, more specifically, the mitochondria—the powerhouse portion of the cells—are the "cleaning crew" in our body. If the office is open from seven to midnight, the mitochondria have less time to do their job ridding the body of dangerous free radicals, inflammation, and culprits of cancer and brain, cardiovascular, and heart disease.

This diet is remarkable because I was not only able to finally lose the weight, quickly and almost effortlessly, but I also never felt deprived. The 8-hour diet does not limit calories or any specific food. It simply limits the time of food consumption. David Zinczenko states that people do not have to follow the 8-hour diet plan each day of the week. In fact, he promises weight loss and health benefits following the plan a mere three days of the week. Of course, your results would be faster and more dramatic the more days of the week you subscribe to the 8:16 eat and fast plan.

By intermittent fasting at least three days a week, you not only naturally cut out excessive calories, but you also enable your body sufficient time to do a daily and crucial overhaul. Studies have shown that one of the primary benefits of intermittent fasting is successful fat loss. The glycogen or blood sugar stores in the liver are usually depleted during the sixteen-hour fast, which in turn signals the body to target fat as an energy source. This is important because traditional dieting causes muscle loss, which leads to other problems and a high probability of gaining the weight back. Fat loss is the real loss we are all aiming for. Fasting also promotes the increase of the human growth hormone, which is responsible for keeping us from some of the devastating effects of aging, including muscle loss, heart disease, mental slowing, diabetes, cancer, and wrinkles.

Notes

1. Research found in David Zinczenko, *The 8-Hour Diet* (New York: Rodale, 2012).

Tips and Advice for Successful Weight Loss

8-Hour Eating Schedule

The foundation of this diet is based on fasting for sixteen hours and eating for eight hours for at least three days out of the week. Following this one thing is imperative in order to realize the weight-loss results and health benefits prescribed in this plan. If you make no other change in your dietary or exercise habits and follow an 8:16 schedule, researchers have noted that you will still see improvements in your body and health. Making a lot of lifestyle changes all at once is difficult, so start with baby steps. But put first things first—intermittent fasting is number one on the list.

Diet is 80 Percent of Weight-Loss Results

Research has found that diet makes up as high as 80 percent of weight-loss results with exercise being 20 percent of results. This is unfortunate for exercise and food lovers. This one realization, aside from abiding to the 8:16 eating-to-fasting ratio, is your greatest ally in losing weight. Another

helpful nugget of information that saw me through hunger pains and food temptations is this: When you feel hungry, that is your body going into its fat stores and feeding itself. Rather than wallow in your misery as your stomach churns, repeat this as a mantra in your mind. It is the affirmation I use to push through times when I am tempted to break the fast early or eat late. Also, rest assured that hunger pains usually only last ten minutes. So do something—besides eating—to distract you. Go for a short walk, work on a project, call a friend, run an errand, and so on. Did you know that exercise is an appetite suppressant? A brief workout not only builds muscle and contributes to cardiovascular fitness, but it will also help you stave off hunger and overeating. That is a triple bonus!

Hydrate

The hypothalamus is the center of the brain that controls hunger and thirst. As a result, when our body interprets hunger, it may actually be thirst. So when you think you are hungry, drink first. Liquid also creates volume in our stomach, so we will likely consume less food. Dr. Brenda Davy claims that, in a study, "people who drank two cups of water right before eating a meal ate between 75 and 90 fewer calories during the meal."[1] In addition, every function of our body needs water to work properly. Drink approximately ten cups of water per day. Ideally drink water before each meal and begin the day with two glasses of ice water with a few drops of fresh lemon juice. The ice-cold water aids in weight loss because we burn calories trying to warm our body. The lemon juice makes your body more alkaline. An alkaline pH is ideal for weight loss.

Cut-Off Time

Through sad experience and trial and error, I have proved the principle of "eat late, gain weight." Even when I subscribed to a form of intermittent fasting, I did not see the results when I ate one big meal late into the evening. But two things can be gleaned from my foolery: 1) You can't beat off a bad diet. 2) You can't eat late and lose weight, even if your calories are within a reasonable range. With that said, six o'clock is the ideal cut-off time and eight o'clock is the latest. My personal eating cut-off time averages around seven o'clock (it's about family logistics).

Exercise in the Morning

You have plenty of good reasons to exercise in the morning, but the most important one is that you are maximizing your weight-loss efforts and tapping into the last of the glycogen stores in your liver for energy. Once those glycogen stores are depleted, your body goes into fat-burning mode. In other words, if you have followed the 8:16 eating plan—if you did not eat a large amount of food late—your body is forced to use fat as fuel. This is exactly what you want. According to David Zinczenko, to be successful on this plan you don't need much more than eight minutes of exercise each morning. However, as an exercise buff, I averaged an hour of exercise each morning. You may ask, "Why in the world would I exercise that much when 80 percent of our weight loss is due to diet?" Even though that statistic is sadly true, exercise still burns calories and increases metabolism, aids in digestion, improves mood and health, distracts from eating, suppresses appetite, and makes you strong and healthy. So if you have the time, exercise more than eight minutes. If not, no worries. A few minutes in the morning is sufficient if your diet is good and is within the eight-hour schedule.

Don't Drink Your Calories

If you are looking for a surefire way to sabotage your weight-loss results, then drink your calories. The last thing you want to do is put down extra calories in the form of liquid. Soda pop, fruit juice, punch, sugary smoothies made from sherbet and "juice" are all bad choices. Even 100 percent juices are too calorie dense. You are better off eating the real fruit. Eat the apple; skip the juice. If you do this, you will get all the nutrients, vitamins, water, and fiber you need, and you'll skip the concentrates and extra calories your body does not need.

Another reason to get your calories from solid food is because it helps you feel sated or full. When we chew, swallow, and release gastric juices we are participating in the digestive process. We are putting forth some effort, and there are chemical responses or processes that are triggered in the brain that helps us feel satisfied and full quicker, and we actually burn more calories with all that hard work. Chew more; burn more.

Adequate Sleep

Our circadian or sleep rhythms are connected to weight loss. Studies have shown that lack of sleep may contribute to less weight loss. When we are sleeping, our body is not only doing a tremendous and important repair work, it is also aiding our bodies in weight loss. So go ahead and indulge in a daily afternoon nap. Set your timer for a fifteen- to twenty-minute refresher and you will not only speed weight loss, but you will also have more energy and stamina during your day without causing sleeping problems at night. Good news.

Mix It Up

You've heard this tip before, but it bares repeating: mix up your diet and exercise every now and then. If you eat the same foods, at the same time each day, your body will get accustomed to that and won't be as efficient in burning calories. When we mix it up with either caloric intake or varying types of activities, then we keep our body guessing without halting progress. It will continue to burn calories instead of storing them and will build muscles. This is especially important if you hit a plateau. Ask any athlete—they will tell you that cross-training or changing their usual workout helps them improve their performance. When we mix up exercise, we use different muscles and create "muscle confusion."

We don't want to get in a weight rut either. When weight loss seems to have slowed to a stall, it is time to evaluate your diet and mix it up. This may mean refraining from intermittent fasting two to three days out of the week or adding a few more complex carbohydrates or lean proteins in your meals. If you have a week or two where you are not following the 8:16 prescribed plan, it's fine; you are mixing it up, not sabotaging your diet. We all need a break sometimes. Just get back on the plan, and you will see results again.

Slow and Steady

Not only am I a tortoise-type runner, but I am also a tortoise-like weight-loss champion, yet that is okay. Actually, it is more than okay. It is A-okay. Slow and steady wins the race. I know this firsthand. By continually putting one foot in front of the other, you will eventually make it to the finish line, in road races as well as weight loss. Like me, you have probably read that losing two to three pounds a week is desirable, doable, and healthy weight loss. Any faster and you are looking at something radical, dangerous, or scary. Scientific studies show that slow weight loss is *real* and often permanent weight loss. Who doesn't want that? Temporary weight loss is not on the agenda now or ever. Slow, sustained weight reduction and subsequent weight management is vital. Be consistent in your efforts, no matter how small, and you will consistently shrink in size.

Notes

1. Bill Hendrick, "Water May Be Secret Weapon in Weight Loss," WebMD, August 23, 2010, http://www.webmd.com/diet/news/20100823/water-may-be-a-secret-weapon-in-weight-loss.

Skinny-licious Recipes 《《《《《《《《《《《《《《

Eating the food in this book will speed up weight-loss results by leaps and bounds without sacrificing taste and family appeal. The recipes are quick, easy, and family-friendly. One-dish meals are particularly helpful in getting the most nutrition with the least amount of calories and investment of time. You might notice that I have included several soup, salad, and sandwich recipes in this cookbook. This is not because it is necessary to eat like a rabbit on the 8-hour diet but because they are tasty and effective in shedding unwanted weight. Eating plenty of soups, salads, and sandwiches with lean meats and a variety of vegetables ensures vitamins, minerals, and nutrients are included and consumed while on this diet.

You might also note the lack of breakfast or bread sections. First, breakfast will typically be skipped while subscribing to the 8-hour diet, but that does not mean that breakfast foods should be avoided while on this eating plan. Breakfast burritos, oatmeal, and eggs are excellent foods to consume within the eight-hour eating period. Second, bread, though permissible, is not helpful in losing extra pounds efficiently and quickly. So recipes for these foods will be limited.

I believe in the "Power of the Mom." Since I have chosen to cook lighter fare and model good exercise habits, my husband has lost twenty-five pounds in three months and my already trim seventeen- and nineteen-year-old children have each lost fifteen pounds while gaining shapely muscle. This has not only been a personal transformation, but a family one as well. The principles in this simple diet have proven effective for all the people I know who have tried it in addition to people I have read about.

Seeing consistent weight loss is empowering. You finally have hope for a healthier, leaner body and a better, more productive, and longer life. We all want what is best for our families and ourselves. This personal achievement has given me a new lease on life with the health benefits alone. However, vanity played a part too. Feeling good in my clothes, sliding into a size-six pair of jeans and a small top, is exhilarating to say the least. We all want to look *and* feel good. Follow this diet plan and enjoy these recipes, and you too will experience a slimmer you!

lunch

ORANGE BANANA SMOOTHIE

Serves 4

This yummy smoothie is an excellent source of calcium and protein.

16 oz. Greek fruit yogurt

**1 cup fresh orange juice
(not from concentrate)**

1 banana

1 scoop vanilla-flavored whey protein

2 cups fresh fruit

directions ....

1. In a blender, combine ingredients and pulse until smooth.

1 serving
  8 tbs
  1/4 cup
  1/4 banana

1 tsp

1/2 cup fruit

MANGO PEACH SMOOTHIE

Mango and peach are complementary fruits. They blend well together and enhance one other. This smoothie is also a great source of vitamin A and tastes like an Orange Julius. It is creamy and refreshing.

Serves
6

1 cup vanilla or peach Greek yogurt

1 cup frozen peaches

1 cup frozen mangoes

8 oz. peach juice

1 cup fresh orange juice
(not from concentrate)

1 Tbsp. ground flax seed

directions

1. Puree ingredients in a blender.

2.5 tbsps yogurt

1 serving

1/2 tsp ground flax see

GREEN SMOOTHIE

Serves 6

Smoothies are a great way to combine yogurt and fruit into a delicious drink packed with calcium antioxidants.

1 cup strawberry yogurt

1 cup vanilla Greek yogurt

2 cups fresh orange juice (not from concentrate)

1 banana

1 cup frozen peaches

1 cup frozen raspberries

4 frozen strawberries

½ cup fresh spinach leaves, washed

directions

1. Place all ingredients in a blender and puree.

GRANOLA AND YOGURT PARFAITS

Parfaits combine several super foods including yogurt, fresh fruit, nuts, and oats.

4 cups old-fashioned rolled oats

½ cup brown sugar

½ cup sweetened coconut flakes

½ cup chopped pecans

½ cup raw pumpkin seeds

½ cup sesame seeds

½ cup raw sunflower seeds

¼ cup oat bran

1 tsp. cinnamon

1 tsp. real vanilla extract

½ cup canola oil

1 cup honey

6 cups vanilla Greek yogurt

4 cups chunked fresh fruit of choice (mangoes, blackberries, strawberries)

directions ●

1. In a large bowl, combine all ingredients except yogurt and fruit. Stir to combine.

2. Spread granola mixture onto a greased cookie sheet and bake in 300-degree oven for 20 minutes.

3. Let cool.

4. In a dessert cup, layer ½ cup vanilla Greek yogurt, followed by ½ cup fresh fruit and then ¼ cup vanilla yogurt. Top with ⅓ cup homemade granola.

CLASSIC DEVILED EGGS

Serves 12

Deviled eggs are a wonderful protein snack. Pair this with fruit and you have a lite and healthy lunch.

12 large hard-boiled eggs

¼ cup mayonnaise

¼ cup sour cream

2 Tbsp. apple cider vinegar

2 tsp. Dijon mustard

½ tsp. salt

¼ tsp. pepper

fresh herbs, like dried parsley, for garnish

directions

1. Cut eggs in half lengthwise.

2. Pop out egg yolks and place in a medium bowl.

3. Add mayonnaise, sour cream, vinegar, mustard, salt, and pepper to egg yolks.

4. Mash or puree in a food processor until mixture is smooth.

5. Snip ½ inch from corner of a ziplock bag and spoon egg mixture into bag.

6. Carefully pipe egg mixture into hollow of each egg yolk. Garnish with herbs.

7. Store in refrigerator, covered, until ready to serve.

ENDIVE SALAD
WITH BALSAMIC VINAIGRETTE

Serves 4

Endive salad calls for few ingredients but boasts bold flavor and is nutrient dense. Delicious.

2 cups endives; washed, dried, and cut into chunks

1 cup arugula, washed and dried

½ cup crumbled bleu cheese

½ cup pecan pieces

Balsamic Vinaigrette Dressing (recipe follows)

directions

1. In a medium bowl, combine endive, arugula, bleu cheese, and pecan pieces.

2. Just before serving, toss with balsamic vinaigrette.

BALSAMIC VINAIGRETTE DRESSING

¼ cup balsamic vinegar

1 tsp. sugar

2 cloves garlic, crushed

½ tsp. salt

½ tsp. fresh ground black pepper

directions

1. Add all ingredients to a jar with a lid.

2. Shake to blend.

CAPRESE SALAD

This fresh-tasting, simple salad is especially good when tomatoes are in season. If you want to create a caprese sandwich instead of a salad, add a toasted baguette slice rubbed with a clove of garlic and brushed with olive oil to each serving. This is a lite and luscious lunch item.

2 large, firm ripe tomatoes, cut into
   ¼-inch slices *½ cup*

½ lb. fresh mozzarella cheese, cut
   into ¼-inch slices *2 ounces*

¹/₈ cup olive oil

2 Tbsp. balsamic vinegar

½ tsp. fresh ground black pepper

¼ tsp. sea salt

½ cup fresh basil leaves

directions ·······································

1. On 4 serving plates, divide tomatoes and mozzarella cheese equally.

2. Divide and drizzle olive oil and vinegar over tomatoes and cheese on plates.

3. Divide and sprinkle pepper and salt over tomatoes and cheese.

3. Garnish with basil leaves.

4. Serve immediately.

SHRIMP COCKTAIL SAUCE

Serves
4

There might not be a slimmer fresh lunch choice than shrimp cocktail.

1 cup ketchup

1 Tbsp. creamy horseradish sauce

16 cooked jumbo shrimp

lemon wedges

directions

1. In a small bowl, combine ketchup and horseradish sauce.

2. Serve with chilled shrimp and lemon wedges.

MISO SOUP

When I go to my favorite sushi restaurant, I often order savory miso soup. I don't think there is a more basic, simple soup. It is lite but still packs an immunity-boosting punch.

Serves
4

4 cups water

1 (8-oz.) pkg. dashi granules (found in Asian section of grocery store)

3 Tbsp. miso paste

1 (8-oz.) pkg. silken tofu, diced into 1-inch cubes

2 green onions, diced

1-inch strip of seaweed, cut into ½-inch pieces

directions

1. In a medium saucepan over medium-high heat, combine water and dashi granules and bring to a boil.

2. Reduce heat to medium, whisk in miso paste, and stir in tofu.

3. Add green onions and seaweed. Simmer for 2 minutes.

4. Serve warm.

CALIFORNIA SUSHI ROLLS

Serves
4

Surprisingly, even children like sushi. Don't be afraid to intro-duce this Eastern staple to your child. It is low calorie and incredibly weight-loss friendly with the nori sheets. Studies have found that seaweed helps the thyroid to function properly.

3 cups sticky rice, cooked

2 nori sheets

½ cup finely chopped cooked crab

1 avocado; peeled, seeded, and chopped into small cubes

2 Tbsp. sesame seeds

soy sauce

wasabi

directions ·······························

1. Place nori sheets shiny side up on a piece of wax paper or sushi rolling mat and sprinkle with sesame seeds.

2. Divide and spread the rice thinly and evenly over the sheets.

3. Divide and place the avocado and crab meat vertically down the middle of each sheet.

4. Roll the nori sheets tightly and cut each into 6 sushi pieces.

5. Serve with soy sauce and wasabi.

CAESAR SALAD WRAPS

Wraps are super foods for families on the go. They travel and store well, are finger foods, and taste good.

Serves 6

¼ cup creamy Caesar dressing

2 spinach tortillas

6 slices mesquite smoked deli turkey breast

4 slices provolone cheese

4 romaine lettuce leaves

1 tomato, sliced thin

directions

1. Spread dressing equally on each tortilla.

2. Divide and layer turkey, cheese, lettuce, and tomato on each tortilla.

3. Roll tortillas and cut into 2-inch pieces.

BERRY GREEN SALAD
WITH POPPY SEED DRESSING

**Serves
12**

This salad is not only beautifully colorful, but it is loaded with antioxidants and flavor. The crushed cinnamon almonds is a surprise seasoning that complements this salad in a wonderful way. Pair this with a savory wrap or sandwich, and you will have a tasty and nutritious superstar!

1 head romaine lettuce,
   cut into 1½-inch chunks

1 cup red leaf lettuce, broken into
   medium pieces

1 cup fresh strawberries; washed,
   dried, and sliced

1 cup blackberries, washed and dried

1 cup thinly sliced red onion

1 cup shredded mozzarella cheese

1 cup crushed Roasted Cinnamon
   Almonds (p. 142)

1 cup Poppy Seed Dressing
   (recipe follows)

directions ·

1. In a large bowl, combine all ingredients except for almonds and dressing.

2. Just before serving, toss salad with almonds and dressing.

POPPY SEED DRESSING

¾ cup canola oil

⅓ cup red wine vinegar

⅓ cup sugar

1 tsp. dry mustard

½ tsp. salt

¼ tsp. fresh ground pepper

1 Tbsp. poppy seeds

directions ··

1. Add all ingredients in a glass jar with a lid.

2. Secure lid and shake to combine.

3. Serve over Berry Green Salad.

TURKEY CRANBERRY WRAPS

Serves
4

In honor of my turkey-junkie husband, I created this wrap. The day after Thanksgiving, my father and my husband love to make turkey and cranberry sandwiches with the leftover meat. Why wait for The fourth Thursday in November to roll around to enjoy these flavors when you can make a turkey cranberry wrap year round.

¼ cup mayonnaise

⅛ cup cranberry sauce

2 (8-inch) wheat tortillas

6 slices smoked deli turkey breast

4 slices provolone cheese

4 red leaf lettuce leaves, washed and dried

1 small tomato, sliced thin

directions

1. Divide and spread mayonnaise and cranberry sauce over tortillas.

2. Divide and layer turkey, cheese, lettuce, and tomatoes on tortillas.

3. Roll up tortillas and cut into 2-inch pieces.

BUFFALO CHICKEN WRAPS

Serves
8

If you are a fan of buffalo wings with ranch dip, then you are going to love these Buffalo Chicken Wraps. This wrap starts with buffalo seasoned deli chicken. It is finished with the spicy ranch dressing. This wrap is a favorite with men, women, and children. This is a perfect lunch wrap.

¼ cup ranch dressing

1 tsp. spicy chicken wing sauce

2 (8-inch) flour tortillas

6 slices deli buffalo chicken breast

¼ cup crumbled feta cheese

4 romaine lettuce leaves,
   washed and dried

1 medium tomato,
   sliced thin

directions ••

1. In a small bowl, combine ranch dressing with spicy chicken wing sauce.

2. Divide and spread sauce over flour tortillas.

3. Divide and layer chicken, cheese, lettuce, and tomato slices on tortillas.

4. Roll each up each tortilla and then cut into 2-inch pieces.

HAM AND HAVARTI CHEESE WRAPS

My paternal grandmother first introduced me to Havarti cheese. Harvati is a slightly soft, creamy cheese with a mild, almost buttery flavor. It complements the flavors of the applewood ham. This is a twist on classic ham and cheese.

Serves
6

¼ cup mayonnaise

2 Tbsp. honey mustard

2 (8-inch) flour tortillas

6 slices applewood smoked
   deli ham

4 slices Havarti cheese

1 medium tomato,
   cut into thin slices

1 cup butter leaf lettuce
   washed, dried, and chopped
   into large pieces

directions ••

1. Divide and spread mayonnaise and mustard between tortillas.

2. Divide and layer tortillas with ham, cheese, tomato, and lettuce.

3. Roll up tortillas and cut into 2-inch pieces.

COBB SALAD

Serves 6

Who says salads are chick food? Cobb salad is my hunky husband's favorite salad. I think the bacon and eggs—two of his favorite breakfast foods—have something to do with it. However, not only do the bacon, eggs, and cheese add flavor, but they also add protein.

2 cups chunked iceberg lettuce

2 cups chunked romaine lettuce

½ cup pealed and shredded carrots

½ cup shredded red cabbage

1 cup seeded and diced Roma tomatoes

1 cup crisply cooked and crumbled bacon

½ cup shredded mild cheddar cheese

1 cup diced hard-boiled eggs

1 cup croutons

1 cup Homemade Ranch Dressing (p. 33)

directions

1. In a large bowl, combine lettuces, carrots, cabbage, and tomatoes.

2. Just before serving, fold in bacon, cheese, eggs, and croutons. Serve with Homemade Ranch Dressing.

HOMEMADE RANCH DRESSING

Ranch is a favorite American salad dressing. Every home cook should have a homemade ranch dressing recipe on hand. It's great for salads, vegetable platters, wraps, and sandwiches.

Serves
10

1 cup mayonnaise

½ cup buttermilk

¼ cup sour cream

1 tsp. dried parsley

1 tsp. dried dill

1 tsp. dried chives

½ tsp. garlic powder

½ tsp. onion powder

¼ tsp. seasoned salt

¼ tsp. fresh ground
    black pepper

2 tsp. dried parsley

1 tsp. garlic powder

½ tsp. ground pepper

directions •

1. Combine all ingredients in a small bowl.

2. Cover and chill dressing in refrigerator for at least 30 minutes or until thick.

3. Serve over your favorite green salad or use as a dip for fresh cut vegetables.

SUMMER ROLLS
WITH THAI PEANUT SAUCE

Serves 8

I am drawn to ethnic cuisine, including Thai, Indian, Italian, Mexican, Chinese, Japanese, and so on. International cuisine expands our palette with different uses of spices and ingredients. This wonderful lite wrap is elegant with interesting blends of flavor and texture. I love this for ladies' luncheons or summer outdoor gatherings.

1 cup water

8 rice papers

16 shrimp, cooked

1 cup spinach leaves, washed and dried

1 cup bean sprouts

1 cup shredded carrots

1 cup Chinese thread noodles, cooked according to package directions

Thai Peanut Sauce (recipe follows)

directions

1. Pour water in a pie tin.

2. Soak each rice paper one at a time until soft—about 5 seconds.

3. In center of each softened rice paper, place 2 shrimp, 2 spinach leaves, $1/8$ cup bean sprouts, $1/8$ cup carrots, and $1/8$ cup noodles.

4. Fold all four sides in like an envelope.

5. Cut rolls in half and serve with Thai Peanut Sauce.

THAI PEANUT SAUCE:

1 cup creamy peanut butter

1 tsp. soy sauce

¼ cup coconut milk

2 Tbsp. rice vinegar

2 Tbsp. lime juice

2 Tbsp. brown sugar

1 tsp. chili sauce

1 clove garlic

directions

1. Put all ingredients in a blender.

2. Pulse until smooth

3. Serve with Summer Rolls.

WALDORF FRUIT SALAD

**Serves
4**

The Waldorf salad is an American tradition. This is a simple, classy salad to serve for lunch.

2 cups Fuji apples
cored and cut into ½-inch chunks

½ cup thinly chopped celery

1 cup seedless red grapes,
sliced (or ¼ cup raisins)

1 cup chopped walnuts

6 Tbsp. mayonnaise

2 Tbsp. fresh lemon juice

red lettuce leaves, washed
and dried, for garnish

directions ....

1. In a medium bowl, combine apple, celery, grapes, and walnuts.

2. In a small bowl, whisk together mayonnaise and lemon juice.

3. Pour mayonnaise mixture over fruit and fold together.

4. Serve 1 cup of salad on 1 red lettuce leaf.

MEDITERRANEAN CHICKEN SOUP

Mediterranean Chicken Soup is packed with healthy vegetables and spices, making it super weight-loss friendly *and* delicious.

Serves 8

2 Tbsp. olive oil

½ cup finely chopped onions

¼ cup chopped celery

¼ cup chopped zucchini

2 cloves garlic, minced

4 cups chicken broth

1 (14-oz.) can diced tomatoes

¼ cup frozen cut Italian green beans

½ cup peeled and chopped carrots

1 cup water

2 Tbsp. minced fresh parsley

2 tsp. dried oregano

1 tsp. salt

½ tsp. dried basil

¼ tsp. dried thyme

3 cups fresh baby spinach leaves

3 cups shredded cooked chicken

⅓ cup small shell pasta

directions

1. In a skillet, heat olive oil over medium heat.

2. Sauté onions, celery, zucchini, and garlic in oil for 5 minutes or until onions are translucent.

3. Transfer vegetables to a large stockpot and add chicken broth, tomatoes, green beans, carrots, water, parsley, and spices.

4. Bring to a boil, then reduce heat and simmer for 20 minutes.

5. Add spinach leaves, chicken, and pasta and cook for 15 minutes more or until noodles are tender.

HARVEST SALAD

Serves 12

This is *not* the recipe from Ruth's Chris Steak House, but it is the closest I could come to re-creating their wonderful harvest salad. Ruth's Chris Steak House really shines in doing two things: 1) Steaks, and 2) Salads. Their salads are masterpieces of flavors, textures, taste, and creativity. I can't go to their restaurant and not order one of their incredible salads. I should be their spokesperson!

1 cup frozen corn

1 head red leaf lettuce,
 washed and dried

1 small red onion, sliced thin

3 tomatoes, cut into chunks

1 cup dried cherries

1 cup glazed pecans

8 slices cooked bacon, crumbled

½ cup goat cheese
 crumbled into dime-size balls

Vinaigrette Dressing (recipe follows)

directions

1. Spread frozen corn kernels on a greased cookie sheet single layer. Bake in 400-degree oven for 5 minutes or until toasted brown. Let cool.

2. In a large bowl, break lettuce into bite-size pieces. Add corn, onion, tomatoes, cherries, pecans, and bacon. Toss.

3. Just before serving, add goat cheese and toss with Vinaigrette Dressing.

VINAIGRETTE DRESSING

¼ cup apple cider vinegar

3 tsp. brown sugar

2 Tbsp. Dijon mustard

½ cup olive oil

directions •

1. Place all ingredients in a mason jar with a lid and shake until combined.

GREEK SALAD

It's so Greek! This is a nice and traditional Greek salad. It is deliciously savory with the feta cheese and creamy dressing.

1 bunch romaine lettuce,
   cut into large pieces

1 red pepper, seeded and sliced thin

1 small red onion, sliced thin

1 cup crumbled feta cheese

1 cup kalamata olives, pitted

1 cucumber, cut into small chunks

2 cups Creamy Greek Dressing
   (recipe follows)

directions

1. In a large bowl, combine all ingredients except dressing.

2. Just before serving, toss with Creamy Greek Dressing.

CREAMY GREEK DRESSING

½ cup olive oil

2 Tbsp. red wine vinegar

1 tsp. sugar

2 garlic cloves, minced

1 tsp. dried oregano

1 tsp. dried dill weed

dash of salt and black pepper

¾ cup crumbled feta cheese

¾ cup buttermilk

directions ••

1. Combine all ingredients in a blender and puree until thick and creamy.

2. Pour dressing into a bottle with a lid.

3. Place in the refrigerator for 1 hour before serving.

WONTON SALAD

If you are looking for a unique salad, try Wonton Salad. This is a lovely sweet and savory salad with Asian flavors. My daughter had this for breakfast and swooned. She said, "This is the best salad I have ever tasted." Every home cook should have a delicious wonton salad recipe in her repertoire. It has wonderful flavors and varied textures.

1 head green leaf lettuce; washed, dried, and cut into bite-size pieces

3 cups shredded or cubed cooked chicken

1 cup thinly sliced red onions

1 cup chopped green pepper

2 Tbsp. sesame seeds

½ cup raw slivered almonds

2 cups fried wontons (recipe follows)

canola oil for frying

1 cup Sesame Dressing (recipe follows)

directions •

1. In a large salad bowl, combine all ingredients except fried wontons and canola oil, adding dressing last.

2. Right before serving, add fried wontons to salad.

TO MAKE FRIED WONTONS:

1. Heat 2 inches of canola oil in a medium saucepan to 375 degrees.

2. Cut 12 wonton wrappers into four strips about a half inch in width using a pizza cutter.

3. Toss strips of wontons into hot oil until they bubble and turn golden brown. This takes about 1 minute.

SESAME DRESSING

½ cup extra-virgin olive oil

⅓ cup rice vinegar

¼ cup granulated sugar

1 Tbsp. light soy sauce

1 Tbsp. sesame oil

2 cloves garlic, minced

directions ••

1. Place all ingredients in a quart jar with a lid and shake to combine.

CAESAR SALAD

Serves
10

Caesar Salad is a classic recipe that adults and children enjoy. The simple ingredients and savory seasonings makes this a crowd favorite. Homemade croutons and dressing adds a fresh and delightful taste.

1 head romaine lettuce

3 cups grilled chicken strips

Parmesan cheese, shredded

Caesar Salad Dressing (recipe follows)

Homemade Garlic Croutons (recipe follows)

directions •

1. Wash, dry, and cut lettuce into bite-size pieces. Place in salad bowl.

2. Add chicken and Parmesan cheese.

3. Pour dressing over salad and toss. Add croutons just before serving.

CAESAR SALAD DRESSING

If you are anything like me, you prefer Caesar Salad with your Italian food. This recipe is easy yet flavorful and is a nice accompaniment to any Italian dish.

½ cup extra-virgin olive oil

fresh juice and zest from a small lemon

1 tsp. Worcestershire sauce

2 garlic cloves

¼ tsp. fresh black pepper

1 cup Parmesan cheese

directions •

1. Combine all ingredients in blender except for cheese.

2. Stir in cheese last.

HOMEMADE GARLIC CROUTONS

½ baguette

¼ cup olive oil

1 tsp. garlic powder

¼ tsp. black pepper

directions •

1. Cut baguette into ½-inch cubes and set aside.

2. In medium bowl, combine olive oil, garlic powder, and black pepper.

3. Add bread cubes to oil and toss to coat.

4. Bake in 300-degree oven for 5 minutes.

MANGO SPINACH SALAD

Serves 12

Mango Spinach Salad isn't merely a female favorite. My sixteen-year-old son ate three bowls of this "chick" food. I was so pleased!

1 bunch of spinach; washed, dried, and torn into bite-size pieces

½ head of iceberg lettuce, torn into bite size pieces

½ cup thinly sliced fresh mushrooms

1 cup thinly sliced cucumbers, with skin on

2 mangoes; peeled, pitted, and diced

½ cup thinly sliced red onion

6 chicken breasts, grilled and cut into strips (or 1 cooked rotisserie chicken, shredded)

Poppy Seed and Onion Dressing (recipe follows)

directions

1. In a bowl, mix spinach, lettuce, mushrooms, cucumbers, mangoes, and red onion.

2. Add chicken.

3. When ready to serve, pour dressing over salad and toss.

POPPY SEED AND ONION DRESSING

1 Tbsp. poppy seeds

½ cup white wine vinegar

1 cup canola oil

½ cup granulated sugar

¼ of a medium onion, chopped

1 tsp. salt

½ tsp. dry mustard

directions ··

1. Place all ingredients in a quart jar with a lid and shake to combine.

BARBECUE CHICKEN SALAD

Serves 8

Barbecue chicken is one of our family's mainstays. We love it with rice, on salads, or solo. I love freshly made salads with grilled meat. Just ask the guys at Cafe Rio. I suggest making the ranch dressing from scratch, or from the dry mix, because bottled ranch just isn't the same.

2 lbs. chicken tenders

2 cups Sweet Baby Ray's barbecue sauce, plus more

1 head of romaine lettuce, washed and cut into medium pieces

½ cup chopped red pepper

1 cup chopped Roma tomatoes

½ cup chopped red onion

1 can black beans, rinsed and drained

1 cup fresh corn kernels

corn tortilla strips

1 cup Homemade Ranch Dressing (p. 33)

directions

1. Marinate chicken tenders in barbecue sauce for about 20 minutes.

2. Grill chicken on medium heat for about 6 minutes per side, or until no longer pink.

3. In a large bowl, toss lettuce, red pepper, tomatoes, onion, beans, and corn.

4. On six plates, layer salad, chicken, and tortilla strips.

5. Serve with extra barbecue sauce and fresh ranch dressing.

WATERMELON SALAD

Serves 4

While dining at Post 390, a restaurant located in Boston's Back Bay, on our twenty-year anniversary, I enjoyed an amazing watermelon salad. Post 390 is a striking, restored historic post office. The cuisine was outstanding. My husband told our waiter that I was a cookbook author, and they gave us the royal treatment. I toured the kitchen, met the chef, and was photographed with the owner. This is my favorite restaurant to date, and I have dined all over the world. Post 390 serves creative, scrumptious dishes. So if you visit Boston, stop in and enjoy their delicious fare.

2 cups red leaf lettuce washed and broken into large pieces

2 cups green leaf lettuce washed and broken into large pieces

1 cup arugula

16 (1½-inch) pieces of seedless watermelon

½ cup thinly sliced red onion

½ red pepper, chopped into medium chunks

¼ cup English cucumber sliced and cut into half moons

⅓ cup Candied Lemon Zests (recipe follows)

½ cup crumbled feta cheese

½ cup toasted almonds (place sliced almonds on cookie sheet and bake in 350-degree oven for 5 minutes or until golden brown)

Citrus Vinaigrette Dressing (recipe follows)

directions

1. Divide ingredients among four serving plates and drizzle with Citrus Vinaigrette Dressing.

CANDIED LEMON ZESTS:

1 lemon

½ cup sugar

½ cup water

directions ....

1. With a vegetable peeler, remove long strips of zest (without pith) from lemon. Cut into julienne strips.

2. Place in a small saucepan and cover with cold water. Bring to a simmer over medium heat. Cook for 7 minutes and drain.

3. Return the strips to the pan and add sugar and ½ cup water; return to a simmer.

4. Cook over low heat until the zest is translucent and the syrup is slightly thickened, 10–15 minutes.

5. Transfer the zest to wax paper with a slotted spoon and let cool completely.

CITRUS VINAIGRETTE DRESSING:

4 Tbsp. canola oil

1 Tbsp. red wine vinegar

2 tsp. lemon juice

2 tsp. Dijon mustard

1 Tbsp. fresh orange juice

1 Tbsp. honey

¼ tsp. salt

¼ tsp. fresh ground pepper

directions ....

1. Blend all ingredients together.

LOBSTER ROLLS

In Boston, lobster rolls are a quintessential lunch choice. In fact, when you go to Quincy Market, you'll find several food stands serving lobster rolls nestled between common hamburger, pizza, and taco food chains.

Serves
8

½ cup mayonnaise

3 Tbsp. fresh lemon juice

¼ cup finely chopped celery

1 Tbsp. chopped fresh parsley leaves

1 tsp. chopped fresh tarragon

¼ tsp. salt

⅛ tsp. black pepper

1½ lbs. lobster meat, cooked

8 open-faced ciabattini rolls

⅛ cup melted butter

directions ....

1. In a medium bowl, combine mayonnaise, lemon juice, celery, parsley, tarragon, salt, and pepper.

2. Fold in lobster meat.

3. Split hoagie buns, brush with butter, and toast under 400-degree broiler for about 2 minutes or until golden brown.

4. Divide lobster meat mixture among rolls. Serve open faced.

GREEK PASTA SALAD

Serves 16

If you can't get your kids to eat traditional Greek salad, try Greek Pasta Salad. I don't know why, but kids don't categorize something with pasta as adult, healthy food.

1 lb. penne pasta, cooked tender

1 cup shredded cooked chicken, (I use cooked rotisserie chicken)

1 cup kalamata olives, pitted

1 cup cherry tomatoes

1 cup crumbled feta cheese

½ cup English cucumber peeled and cut into chunks

½ cup chopped red onion

1 cup baby spinach, washed and dried

Greek Dressing (recipe follows)

directions

1. Combine all ingredients except dressing in a large bowl.

2. Let salad sit covered in refrigerator for 30 minutes before serving.

3. When serving, pour on Greek Dressing.

GREEK DRESSING

½ cup olive oil

2 Tbsp. red wine vinegar

1 tsp. sugar

1 clove garlic, minced

1 tsp. dried oregano leaves

½ tsp. salt

¼ tsp. fresh ground black pepper

½ cup crumbled feta cheese

¾ cup buttermilk

directions •

1. Combine all ingredients in a blender.

2. Puree until creamy.

ROQUEFORT ENDIVE SALAD

Serves 4

While traveling in Málaga, Spain, I experienced this understated, tasty salad. It is a mild salad that is surprisingly satisfying.

1 avocado, sliced into 6 wedges

endive leaves

romaine lettuce, shredded

bleu cheese, crumbled

1 Tbsp. chopped fresh chives

¼ cup Roquefort Dressing (recipe follows)

directions

1. On a large serving platter, line edge of platter with alternating endive leaves and avocado slices.

2. In center of platter, place lettuce, bleu cheese, and chives. Top with Roquefort dressing.

ROQUEFORT DRESSING:

2½ oz. bleu cheese

3 Tbsp. buttermilk

3 Tbsp. sour cream

2 Tbsp. mayonnaise

2 Tbsp. white wine vinegar

¼ tsp. sugar

⅛ tsp. garlic powder

dash of salt and fresh ground pepper

directions

1. Combine all ingredients in blender and blend until combined.

ZESTY PASTA SALAD

This salad tastes lovely with artisan bread and a cold fruit soup. This is an excellent and quick potluck dish that both kids and adults like.

Serves 16

5 lb. bag curly pasta, cooked tender

1 cup cherry tomatoes

1 cup fresh spinach broken into bite-size pieces

1 bunch green onion, chopped

½ red pepper, seeded and chopped

½ cucumber, peeled and chopped into chunks

¼ cup crumbled feta cheese

⅛–¼ cup quality creamy Italian dressing

directions

1. In a large bowl, combine all ingredients and toss.

GREEK SALAD SANDWICH

Serves 8

My five children request this dish almost weekly. The focaccia bread and dressing make this a unique and tasty sandwich.

1 (12-inch) focaccia bread round

6 slices mesquite smoked deli turkey

2 medium tomatoes, sliced thin

⅓ small red onion, sliced thin

½ cup English cucumber peeled and sliced thin

3 romaine lettuce leaves, washed and dried

¼ cup Greek Dressing (p. 55)

directions

1. Split focaccia bread in half.

2. Layer turkey, tomatoes, onion, cucumbers, and lettuce leaves evenly over inside of one foccacia slice.

3. Just before serving, spread dressing evenly over lettuce. Top with other bread slice.

FRENCH ONION SOUP

French onion soup is loaded with immune-building onions, which are in the allium family. Onions also fight cancer. So pour yourself a warm, delicious bowl of French Onion Soup and know you are doing something nice not only for your taste buds but for your health as well. Serve this soup with toasted baguette bread and shredded mozzarella cheese.

Serves
4

3 Tbsp. butter

1 Tbsp. canola oil

1½ lbs. onions, sliced thin
  (about 5 cups)

¼ tsp. sugar

3 Tbsp. flour

3 (14-oz.) cans beef broth

1 cup water

directions ....

1. In a large stockpot, heat butter and oil on medium heat.

2. Add onions and sugar. Cook slowly, covered, for 15 minutes.

3. Turn down heat and cook for 30 more minutes.

4. Sprinkle flour on top of onions and stir for 3 minutes.

5. Turn off heat and add beef broth and water.

6. Simmer, partially covered, for another 30 minutes.

snacks

CHUNKY GUACAMOLE

Serves 16

Holy guacamole, this is good! Guacamole is an excellent source of heart-healthy plant fat, and it tastes pretty good with tortilla chips, taco soup, and grilled salads.

2 avocados, halved and seeded

$2/3$ cup finely chopped, seeded Roma tomatoes

¼ cup finely sliced green onions

2 Tbsp. fresh lime juice

2 cloves garlic, minced

¼ tsp. salt

$1/8$ tsp. pepper

directions

1. Mash avocados in a medium bowl.

2. Add tomatoes, onions, lime juice, garlic, salt, and pepper.

3. Stir to combine.

KENDRA'S SIMPLE SALSA

This is my sister-in-law's kid-friendly, quick salsa. It is lightning fast to make and mild enough that the kids dig right in. You don't even need to tell them it is packed with lycopenes and cancer-fighting antioxidants. Serve with tortilla chips.

Serves
16

1 (28-oz.) can whole peeled tomatoes, drained (reserve 2 Tbsp. juice)

¾ cup fresh cilantro leaves

1 (4-oz.) can roasted peeled green chilies

⅛ cup chopped green onions

2 Tbsp. tomato juice from can

½ Tbsp. sugar

¾ tsp. garlic powder

¼ tsp. salt

directions

1. Place all ingredients in a blender and pulse until smooth.

CINNAMON SUGAR CHIPS WITH FRUIT SALSA

Serves
8

Cinnamon sugar tortilla chips are a wonderful snack. This is one of my all-time favorite desserts, snacks, appetizers. The combination of flavors and textures is like a south-of-the-border symphony to my taste buds. My kids love this treat. It takes a little effort, but oh boy! It is worth it.

2 cups chopped fresh strawberries

2 cups chopped fresh pineapple

2 cups chopped fresh apples

2 cups chopped fresh peaches
(when in season)

½ cup granulated sugar

2 Tbsp. cinnamon

¼ cup butter, softened

8 flour tortillas

directions

1. Combine fruit in a medium bowl and set aside.

2. Preheat oven to 400 degrees.

3. In a small bowl, combine sugar and cinnamon.

4. Spread ½ tablespoon butter on both sides of each tortilla.

5. Sprinkle 1 tablespoon of sugar mixture over each buttered tortilla and place on large cookie sheet.

6. Bake for 12 minutes, turning tortillas once.

7. Let tortillas cool. Then stack four tortillas together and cut into wedges using pizza cutter. Repeat with remaining tortillas.

8. Serve with fruit salsa.

BLACK BEAN DIP

Serves
12

I love interesting chip dips. Black Bean Dip is easy but incredibly flavorful and savory, and it is a great accompaniment to any Mexican meal. This recipe is not only low carb and an excellent source of plant protein, but it is a fantastic appetizer as well. Beans also contain good-for-you fiber. Serve this dip with fresh cilantro, tortilla chips, and lime wedges.

1 (15-oz.) can black beans, rinsed and drained

1 (4-oz.) can chopped green chilies

¼ cup bottled salsa of choice

½ tsp. ground cumin

½ tsp. garlic powder

directions

1. Combine ingredients in a blender.

2. Pulse until smooth, about 3 minutes.

ORANGE FRUIT DIP

Simple but splendid! Serve with cut-up fresh fruits in season.

Serves
8

1 (8-oz.) pkg. cream cheese, softened

7 oz. marshmallow cream

2 tsp. orange zest

1 Tbsp. fresh orange juice
(not from concentrate)

directions •

1. Using an electric mixer, beat ingredients until smooth.

BRUSCHETTA

Bruschetta is not only packed with lycopenes and antioxidants, but it also boasts bold and fresh flavors and complementary textures. This is a perfect snack, especially if you are craving something Italian.

1 baguette

olive oil

1 (15-oz.) can diced tomatoes, drained

½ cup chopped fresh basil leaves

2 Tbsp. olive oil

3 cloves garlic, minced

½ tsp. fresh ground black pepper

¼ tsp. salt

½ cup fresh grated Parmesan cheese

directions

1. Cut baguette into 1-inch slices. Baste with olive oil and bake in 400-degree oven for 5 minutes to toast.

2. In a medium bowl, combine tomatoes, basil leaves, 2 Tbsp. olive oil, garlic, pepper, and salt.

3. Spoon 1½ tablespoons tomato mixture over each baguette slice.

4. Sprinkle cheese evenly over tomato-topped slices.

dinner

HERB-CRUSTED SALMON

Serves 4

Salmon is an excellent source of omega-3 oil. Americans tend to intake more of the not-so-healthy omega-6 oils. Salmon is brain food. Omega-3 is essential for pregnant women because it helps build healthy brains for their babies. This recipe is one of my favorite ways to prepare salmon. The herbs are a flavorful and healthy sidekick to this already nutritious dish.

4 salmon portions

1/3 cup chopped fresh cilantro

1/3 cup chopped fresh parsley

1/3 cup chopped green onions

1 clove garlic, crushed

1 Tbsp. fresh lemon juice

2 tsp. canola oil

1/4 tsp. salt

1/8 tsp. black pepper

directions

1. Rinse fish and pat dry with paper towels. Set aside.

2. In a medium bowl, combine cilantro, green onions, garlic, lemon juice, oil, salt, and pepper.

3. Coat both sides of salmon portions with the herb mixture.

4. Cook salmon on an uncovered grill rack over medium hot coals for 6–9 minutes or until the salmon flakes with a fork.

SEAFOOD STEW

This is a unique and tasty stew. The halibut makes this dish low cal and low fat. It is loaded with vegetables and mild seasonings. Pair this with crusty sourdough bread and a green salad for a wonderful lite dinner.

Serves
6

2 Tbsp. olive oil, divided

1 Tbsp. fresh lime juice

¼ tsp. salt

⅛ tsp. pepper

1 lb. halibut filets,
   cut into 1-inch cubes

1 cup minced onion

1 cup chopped green pepper

½ jalapeño pepper, seeded and
   minced

2 cloves garlic, crushed

1 (14-oz.) can diced tomatoes with
   lime and cilantro, undrained

½ cup unsweetened coconut milk

2 Tbsp. fresh cilantro leaves

3 cups cooked rice

directions

1. In a medium bowl, stir together 1 tablespoon olive oil, lime juice, salt, and pepper. Add cubed fish and toss to coat. Set aside.

2. In a skillet, add remaining oil and heat on medium heat. Add onion, green pepper, jalapeño pepper, and garlic. Cook until tender, about 4 minutes.

3. Stir in undrained tomatoes, coconut milk, and cilantro. Bring to a boil.

4. Reduce heat and simmer, uncovered, for 10 minutes.

5. Stir in fish. Return to a boil. Reduce heat and simmer for 5 minutes or until fish flakes with a fork.

6. Serve over hot rice.

APRICOT CHICKEN

Apricot Chicken is a delicious sweet and savory dish. You can also prepare this in a slow cooker.

¾ cup French salad dressing

¾ cup apricot-pineapple preserves

1 (1.5-oz.) packet onion soup mix

8 chicken breasts, cut in half

directions ·····································

1. Preheat oven to 350 degrees.

2. Combine dressing, preserves, and soup mix in a small bowl.

3. Place chicken in a 9×13 greased dish.

4. Pour sauce over chicken and bake, uncovered, for 50–60 minutes or until chicken is no longer pink.

CLASSIC LASAGNA

This dish isn't fancy or different, but it is classic and delicious. The lean hamburger, cottage cheese, and mozzarella cheese add a significant amount of protein. The tomatoes add antioxidants. Together, this is a one-dish meal that moms can feel good about.

Serves 12

1 lb. extra-lean ground beef

1 (32-oz.) can crushed tomatoes, undrained

1 (6-oz.) can tomato paste

2 cloves garlic, crushed

2 tsp. dried basil

½ tsp. salt

¼ tsp. sugar

3 cups low-fat, small-curd cottage cheese

½ cup fresh grated Parmesan cheese

2 Tbsp. dried parsley leaves

½ tsp. black pepper

6 lasagna noodles, cooked tender

1 lb. mozzarella cheese, shredded

directions •

1. Brown ground beef in a large skillet. Add tomatoes, tomato paste, garlic, basil, salt, and sugar. Stir to combine.

2. Simmer for 15 minutes.

3. In a medium bowl, combine cottage cheese, Parmesan cheese, parsley, and black pepper. Set aside.

4. In a 9×13 dish, layer 3 lasagna noodles, half of cottage cheese mixture, half of mozzarella cheese, and half of meat mixture. Repeat layering in same order with remaining ingredients.

5. Bake in 350-degree oven for 30 minutes. Let stand 10 minutes before serving.

SPICY THAI CHICKEN SOUP

Serves 6

Spicy Thai Chicken Soup is delicious, but it is spicy. Spices rev up the metabolism and satisfy our pallets in such a way that it cuts our sugar cravings. I like to heat things up with spices, but if your family wants something more mellow, pass on the jalapeño.

1 Tbsp. canola oil

½ cup finely chopped onion

3 cloves garlic, minced

½ fresh jalapeño pepper,
  seeded and finely chopped

1 Tbsp. minced fresh ginger

2 (10-oz.) cans diced tomatoes with
  lime juice and cilantro, undrained

2 cups chicken broth

3 cups shredded cooked chicken
  (I use rotisserie)

½ cup unsweetened coconut milk

½ cup fresh cilantro

½ cup fresh parsley

1 Tbsp. fresh lime juice

½ tsp. black pepper

¼ tsp. salt

3 cups cooked short-grain rice

directions

1. In a skillet, heat oil on medium heat.

2. Add onion, garlic, jalapeño, and ginger. Cook until tender, about 4 minutes.

3. Transfer onion mixture to a large stockpot and add tomatoes, chicken broth, shredded chicken, coconut milk, cilantro, parsley, lime juice, pepper, and salt.

4. Turn heat to low and simmer for 5 minutes.

5. Serve over cooked rice.

BLEU CHEESE SLIDERS

Serves
6

The secret to this dish is keeping the bread to a minimum. With a juicy meat patty, bleu cheese, and fresh vegetable toppings, the bun distracts. So why not lose the top bun or use a dinner roll? Sliders are men-pleasers, but women and children like them too.

1 lb. extra-lean ground beef

1 tsp. Worcestershire sauce

about ¾ cup crumbled bleu cheese,
  divided

½ tsp. salt

¼ tsp. black pepper

mayonnaise

2 ripe tomatoes, sliced

iceberg lettuce

½ red onion, sliced

6 fresh dinner rolls, cut in half

directions

1. In a medium bowl, mix beef, Worcestershire sauce, ½ cup bleu cheese, salt, and pepper. Form 6 patties.

2. Grill on medium heat for 3–4 minutes per side or until no longer pink.

3. Assemble sliders by adding mayonnaise, cooked patty, bleu cheese, tomato, lettuce leaf, and onion on one half of a dinner roll. Top with other dinner roll half.

SHRIMP PORTOFINO

Since the time I was in grade school, I loved shrimp. This is a popular Italian dish. It is lite and satisfying served over pasta.

Serves
6

3 Tbsp. olive oil

3 cloves garlic, crushed

30 shrimp, deveined and shelled with
   tails on

¼ cup butter

8 oz. fresh button mushrooms, sliced

2 cups heavy cream

½ cup fresh lemon juice

2 Tbsp. chopped fresh parsley

1 tsp. salt

½ tsp. dried oregano

¼ tsp. black pepper

2 cups fresh baby spinach leaves,
   washed and dried

½ cup raw pine nuts

1 lb. angel-hair pasta, cooked tender

directions •

1. In a large skillet, heat oil over medium heat. Add garlic and stir for 30 seconds or until golden.

2. Add shrimp and cook until pink and no longer opaque, about 4 minutes.

3. Remove shrimp and set aside.

4. In the same skillet over medium heat, melt butter, place mushrooms, and cook for 5 minutes or until browned. Add cream, lemon juice, parsley, salt, oregano, pepper, shrimp, spinach leaves, and pine nuts.

5. Cook until spinach just begins to melt.

6. In a large serving bowl, toss shrimp mixture with noodles. Serve warm.

CHICKEN COCONUT CURRY

It's true—I'm in love with curry! I make this excellent recipe often. My family loves it, and it is not only packed with flavor, but it is also healthy, lite, and quick!

2 Tbsp. olive oil

1 cup chopped onion

½ jalepeño pepper, seeded and minced

1 red bell pepper, chopped

2 Tbsp. fresh ginger peeled and finely minced

1 (15-oz.) can chicken broth

2 (10-oz.) cans diced tomatoes with lime and cilantro, undrained

2 (14-oz.) cans unsweetened coconut milk

4 tsp. red curry powder

3 cups cooked chicken (I use rotisserie)

3 Tbsp. fresh lime juice

½ tsp. salt

¼ tsp. black pepper

1 cup chopped fresh cilantro

3 cups cooked sticky rice

directions

1. In a large skillet, heat oil on medium heat. Sauté onion, jalepeño pepper, and red pepper until tender, about 4 minutes. Add ginger the last minute of cooking.

2. Transfer onion mixture to a large stockpot and add chicken broth, diced tomatoes, coconut milk, curry powder, chicken, lime, salt, pepper, and cilantro.

3. Turn heat to low and simmer for 5 minutes.

4. Serve over rice.

...SHEW CHICKEN

Just about any recipe with cashews is a favorite dish of mine. Cashews impart a different texture and lovely flavor to chicken dishes. Slightly spicy and tangy, this recipe is not only a favorite menu item at Chinese restaurants, but it is also a requested dish at home.

¼ cup olive oil

4 chicken breasts,
   cut into 2-inch pieces

1 cup finely chopped onion

2 garlic cloves, crushed

1 green pepper, cut into strips

2 Tbsp. fresh ginger

Spicy Cashew Chicken Sauce
   (recipe follows)

1½ cups salted cashews

4 cups cooked rice

directions ....

1. In a sauté pan, heat oil on medium heat.

2. Add chicken pieces and brown all sides, about 4 minutes.

3. Add onion, garlic, pepper, and ginger. Cook until onion and pepper are tender, about 4 minutes more.

4. Turn heat to low and let simmer while preparing sauce.

5. Add sauce to chicken mixture. Add cashews and cook for 1 more minute.

6. Serve over cooked rice.

SPICY CASHEW CHICKEN SAUCE

½ cup chicken broth

½ cup ketchup

4 tsp. soy sauce

2 Tbsp. Worcestershire sauce

3 Tbsp. sugar

½ tsp. salt

1½ tsp. sesame oil

¼ tsp. cayenne pepper

directions •

1. Combine all ingredients in a medium bowl.

TARRAGON ORANGE HALIBUT

Serves
6

The Chef's Table restaurant serves a similar dish to this. When I dine at this fine establishment, this is the item I usually order. It is creamy and tangy with the citrus juices and zests.

6 halibut portions

1 tsp. lemon zest

1 tsp. orange zest

½ cup fresh squeezed orange juice, divided

¼ cup fresh squeezed lemon juice

½ tsp. tarragon

1 cup cream

½ cup vegetable broth

2 Tbsp. cornstarch

salt and pepper to taste

¼ tsp. paprika

directions •••

1. Preheat oven to 400 degrees.

2. Place halibut in a greased 9×13 baking dish and set aside.

3. In a medium bowl, combine citrus zests, ¼ cup orange juice, lemon juice, and tarragon. Cook in a saucepan over low heat.

4. Gently whisk in cream and vegetable broth.

5. Dissolve cornstarch in ¼ cup orange juice and add to sauce.

6. Cook and stir until thickened.

7. Pour sauce over halibut. Sprinkle with salt, pepper, and paprika. Bake for 20 minutes.

HARVEST GARDEN CHILI

Serves
12

Harvest chili is so robust, you will not miss the meat. When I make this chili, it garners many compliments from men and women alike. I love homemade chili with cornbread and apple juice.

½ cup olive oil, divided

1 small zucchini, washed and cut into chunks

1 small banana squash, washed and cut into chunks

2 onions, chopped

4 cloves garlic, crushed

1 large red bell pepper, chopped

1 large green bell pepper, chopped

2 (32-oz.) cans crushed tomatoes, undrained

2 Tbsp. chili powder

1 Tbsp. each of cumin, basil, dried oregano, and dried dill weed

2 tsp. fresh ground black pepper

1 tsp. salt

1½ tsp. fennel seeds

½ cup finely chopped fresh parsley

1 (15-oz.) can kidney beans, drained

1 (15-oz.) can black beans, drained

2 Tbsp. fresh lemon juice

sour cream

directions ....

1. Heat ¼ cup olive oil in a skillet over medium heat. Add zucchini and squash.

2. Sauté until tender, about 6 minutes.

3. Transfer to a large stockpot.

4. Heat remaining ¼ cup oil in the skillet over low heat. Add onions, garlic, and bell peppers. Sauté until tender, about 8 minutes. Transfer to the pot.

5. Turn heat to low. Add tomatoes, chili powder, cumin, basil, oregano, pepper, salt, fennel, and parsley. Cook uncovered, stirring often, for 30 minutes.

6. Stir in beans, dried dill weed, and lemon juice and cook for another 15 minutes.

7. Serve with sour cream.

BRUSCHETTA CHICKEN

Serves
8

At the Cheesecake Factory, my husband always orders the Tuscan chicken. This recipe is my attempt to create a similar dish.

salt and pepper

4 chicken breasts, split in half

¼ cup olive oil

2 cloves garlic, minced

½ cup chopped onion

1 (15-oz.) can diced tomatoes, drained

1 cup canned artichoke hearts drained and quartered

2 Tbsp. capers

¼ cup balsamic vinegar

½ tsp. salt

¼ tsp. fresh ground pepper

⅛ cup fresh basil leaves, chopped

¼ cup fresh grated Parmesan cheese

directions ···

1. Salt and pepper chicken breasts.

2. On medium coals, grill chicken until no longer pink, about 7 minutes per side.

3. In a skillet, heat olive oil on medium heat.

4. Add garlic and onion. Cook until tender.

5. Add tomatoes, artichoke hearts, capers, balsamic vinegar, salt, and pepper. Simmer for 5 minutes.

6. To serve, divide bruschetta mixture among chicken breasts. Sprinkle with fresh basil leaves and Parmesan cheese.

GRILLED LIME CILANTRO SHRIMP SKEWERS

Barbecuing brings out the best in shrimp. The lime cilantro marinade is an excellent seasoning for fish. Enjoy this lite, low-fat, low-carb dinner.

Serves
4

¼ cup canola oil

⅛ cup fresh lime juice

1 clove garlic, minced

⅛ cup chopped cilantro

24 medium shrimp, deveined and shelled with tails on

½ tsp. salt

¼ tsp. black pepper

directions •

1. In a medium bowl, combine oil, lime juice, garlic, and cilantro. Add shrimp.

2. Cover and let marinate for 1–2 hours in refrigerator.

3. Use 4 water-soaked wood skewers. Thread 6 shrimp on each skewer. Sprinkle shrimp with salt and pepper.

4. Grill over medium heat for about 3 minutes or until no longer opaque.

GENERAL'S BARBECUE CHICKEN SKEWERS

Barbecue chicken is a family favorite, particularly with a creamy dip and celery ribs. Kids love dipping their food. This is a lean, healthy protein dish with bold barbecue flavor.

Serves **4**

4 boneless chicken breasts

1 (28-oz.) bottle ketchup

½ cup brown sugar

¼ cup Worcestershire sauce

¼ cup apple cider vinegar

2 Tbsp. molasses

1 Tbsp. prepared mustard

spicy ranch dressing for dipping

celery ribs

directions •

1. Cut each chicken breast into four strips.

2. Thread chicken strips on 4 wooden skewers that have soaked in water for 30 minutes.

3. In a medium bowl, combine ketchup, brown sugar, Worcestershire sauce, apple cider vinegar, molasses, and mustard.

4. Reserve one cup of barbecue sauce for dipping.

5. Brush remaining barbecue sauce liberally over each chicken strip.

6. Cook chicken skewers on grill on medium heat for 6–7 minutes per side or until starting to char and no longer pink.

7. Serve with spicy ranch dressing and celery ribs.

BLACKENED HALIBUT
WITH ALASKAN TARTAR SAUCE

A few years ago, my father went on a deep-sea fishing trip to Alaska, where he line-caught salmon and halibut. He freeze-packed the fish and mailed it home. On the boat, he enjoyed fresh fish with the following homemade tartar sauce.

4 tsp. blackened seasoning

2 lbs. halibut cut into 4 portions

1 Tbsp. butter

1 Tbsp. canola oil

8 lemon wedges for garnish

Alaskan Tartar Sauce (recipe follows)

directions •••

1. Sprinkle ½ teaspoon of blackened seasoning over each side of halibut.

2. In a skillet, heat butter and canola oil over medium heat.

3. Pan-sear each side of halibut in the skillet over medium-high heat, about 1 minute on each side.

4. Turn heat to medium-low and cook for about 3 minutes on each side, turning once.

5. Serve with lemon wedges and Alaskan Tartar Sauce.

ALASKAN TARTAR SAUCE

1 cup mayonnaise

¼ cup chopped green onions

1 tsp. lemon pepper

directions ••

1. Combine all ingredients in a small bowl and stir to mix.

STUFFED PEPPERS

Serves 4

When my daughter returned home from Chicago, I served her a stuffed red pepper hot out of the oven. She said, "This is the best thing I've eaten the past week, and I've had some good food!" This is a variation of my mother's recipe that her neighbor Big Ray loved and requested.

1 lb. lean ground beef

1 tsp. crushed garlic

salt and pepper to taste

1 tsp. dried basil leaves

1 Tbsp. canola oil

⅓ cup minced onion

1½ cups cooked white rice

2 (8-oz.) cans tomato sauce, divided

4–5 red bell peppers

directions

1. Brown ground beef in skillet. Add garlic, salt and pepper, and basil.

2. In a small sauté pan, heat oil and onions until onions are soft.

3. In a medium bowl, combine ground beef, onions, and rice.

4. Pour 1½ cups tomato sauce over mixture—reserving ½ cup for tops of stuffed peppers—and stir to combine.

5. Cut one inch off tops of bell peppers and remove seeds.

6. Spoon meat and rice mixture into each pepper. Top each pepper with reserved tomato sauce.

7. Place in deep baking dish. Bake in 350-degree oven for 60 minutes, covered with aluminum foil. Remove foil and bake for 5 more minutes.

SALMON WITH BASIL PESTO BUTTER

Pesto butter complements salmon well—it is buttery and savory.

½ cup butter, softened

1 Tbsp. fresh lemon juice

1 Tbsp. prepared basil pesto

4 salmon portions

4 lemon wedges for garnish

directions •

1. Preheat oven to 400 degrees.

2. In a small bowl, combine butter, lemon juice, and basil pesto.

3. Scoop 1 tablespoon of butter mixture over each salmon portion.

4. Bake, uncovered, for 20 minutes.

5. Serve with lemon wedges.

CHICKEN CORDON BLEU

**Serves
8**

For each of my children's birthdays, I let them choose what they would like me to make for dinner. My son, Jeremy, requested Chicken Cordon Bleu. This dish is especially delicious with mashed potatoes and glazed carrots.

8 slices Swiss cheese

8 boneless chicken breasts

8 pieces thinly sliced chipped beef deli meat

8 strips bacon

16 oz. sour cream

2 (14-oz.) cans cream of chicken soup

directions •

1. Preheat oven to 275 degrees.

2. Place a slice of Swiss cheese on top of each chicken breast.

3. Wrap chicken with chipped beef followed by one strip of bacon.

4. Place wrapped chicken in 9×13 glass dish.

5. In a medium bowl, combine sour cream and cream of chicken soup.

6. Pour mixture evenly over chicken.

7. Bake uncovered for 3 hours.

SHRIMP RED CURRY

Serves
4

Curry recipes are some of my favorites. Shrimp is a lite addition to this savory, healthy dish.

1 Tbsp. olive oil

½ cup onion, sliced thin

½ jalapeño pepper, seeded and minced

½ cup diced red bell pepper

1 clove garlic, minced

1 (14-oz.) can unsweetened coconut milk

4 tsp. red curry powder

½ cup bamboo shoots

1 lb. large shrimp, peeled and deveined

2 cups cooked rice

directions ••

1. In a large skillet, heat oil over medium heat.

2. Sauté onion, jalapeño, red pepper, and garlic until tender, 4–5 minutes.

3. Add coconut milk, curry, bamboo shoots, and shrimp.

4. Cook until shrimp is no longer opaque, 3–5 minutes.

5. Serve over cooked rice.

HEARTY VEGETABLE BEEF SOUP

Move over canned vegetable soup—here comes the real deal! This soup is a nutrition-packed powerhouse. Vegetables, broth, and small amounts of lean meat is a super combination for any meal. This is a delicious one-dish wonder.

Serves
10

½ lb. round steak,
    cut into small 1-inch cubes

2 Tbsp. canola oil

3 (14-oz.) cans beef broth

2 cups picante salsa

2 cups water

3 carrots, peeled and diced

2 garlic cloves, crushed

1 cup peeled and diced
    Yukon Gold potatoes

1 (14-oz.) can green beans, drained

½ cup frozen peas

1 cup fresh spinach leaves, washed

directions

1. In a sauté pan over medium heat, brown steak in oil, turning once, about 5 minutes.

2. In a large stockpot, combine beef broth, salsa, water, carrots, garlic, and steak.

3. Bring to a boil and then turn down to simmer. Simmer for 45 minutes or until meat and carrots are tender.

4. Add potatoes, green beans, peas, and spinach leaves and simmer for another 20 minutes or until potatoes are tender but not mushy and falling apart.

IRISH BEEF STEW

Serves 10

You don't have to be Irish to make or enjoy this scrumptious stew. It is savory and lovely. Notice: there are no potatoes in this recipe. Potatoes tend to leave a starchy flavor in slow-cooked foods such as roasts, stews, and soups. But if you would like to add them, do so in the last 30 minutes of cooking.

1 medium onion, chopped

2 cloves garlic, crushed

3 Tbsp. butter, divided

1 Tbsp. canola oil

1 tsp. salt

½ tsp. black pepper

2 lbs. round steak, cut in 1-inch cubes

2 (15-oz.) cans beef broth

4 cups water, divided

5 large carrots, peeled and cut into 1-inch chunks

1 bouquet garni (instructions follow)

1 (1-oz.) packet brown gravy mix

directions

1. In a skillet, sauté onion and garlic in 2 tablespoons of butter until onions are tender.

2. Add onion mixture to a large stockpot.

3. In the skillet, on medium heat, add remaining butter and canola oil. Salt and pepper beef and brown on all sides, about 6 minutes.

4. In a large stockpot, add beef, broth, 3 cups water, carrots, and bouquet garni.

5. Combine remaining water with dry gravy mix until dissolved and add to stockpot.

6. Cook for 1–2 hours or until carrots and beef are tender. Remove bouquet garni before serving.

For bouquet garni:

Cut a 4-inch square of cheesecloth (find in cooking stores or cooking section of the supermarket) and place 1 tablespoon of dried herbs in center. (Herbes de Provence is a good blend.) Bring corners together and tie with kitchen twine.

CHICKEN TIKKA MASALA

Serves 8

One of our all-time-favorite restaurants is Bombay House, cuisine of India. We always order chicken tikka masala and their wonderful garlic naan. It is likely the best chicken dish I have ever sunk my teeth into. We are regulars there, but I thought it would be a good idea to try to duplicate this dish at home. This recipe is a close second to that of the award-winning Bombay House.

2 Tbsp. olive oil, divided

1 Tbsp. butter

1½ lbs. chicken breast, cut into 2-inch cubes

dash of salt and fresh ground pepper

1 (15-oz.) can crushed tomatoes, undrained

¼ cup chopped cilantro leaves

2 tsp. garam masala seasoning

1 tsp. turmeric

1 medium onion, diced

1 small green pepper, diced

½ jalepeño pepper, finely diced

2 cloves garlic, chopped

½ cup heavy cream

4 cups cooked rice

directions . . . .

1. In a sauté pan, heat 1 tablespoon oil and butter.

2. Add chicken. Season with salt and pepper. Sear on each side on medium-high heat, about 2 minutes.

3. Turn heat to medium-low. Add tomatoes, cilantro leaves, masala, and turmeric.

4. Cover chicken and let simmer for 10 minutes.

5. In another sauté pan, heat 1 tablespoon olive oil on medium heat. Add onion, green pepper, jalapeño pepper, and garlic.

6. Cook until vegetables are tender and then add to chicken mixture. Let simmer for another 10 minutes or until chicken is no longer pink when cut into largest piece.

7. Add heavy cream. Heat through about 2 minutes.

8. Serve over hot cooked rice.

CHICKEN LETTUCE WRAPS

Serves
4

Lettuce wraps are one my favorite Chinese food dishes. I searched for a recipe as close as possible to that of P. F. Chang's. This recipe is somewhat labor intensive, but it is delicious.

1 Tbsp. canola oil

2 boneless skinless chicken breasts

2 Tbsp. soy sauce

2 Tbsp. sugar

½ tsp. rice wine vinegar

1 Tbsp. peanut oil

2 tsp. minced fresh ginger

1 tsp. minced garlic

¼ cup chopped green onions

1 cup water chestnuts, minced

4–5 iceberg lettuce leaves

½ cup prepared chili sauce

Hot Mustard Sauce (recipe follows)

directions

1. Heat canola oil in a skillet on high heat.

2. Sauté chicken breasts for 4–5 minutes per side or until no longer pink.

3. Transfer chicken to a plate to cool.

4. Cut cooled chicken into small pieces.

5. In a small bowl, combine soy sauce, sugar, and rice wine vinegar.

6. Add peanut oil to skillet. Add chicken, ginger, garlic, onions, water chestnuts, and soy sauce mixture.

7. Sauté the mixture for a couple minutes or until heated through. Divide mixture among lettuce cups and serve with prepared chili sauce and Hot Mustard Sauce.

Hot Mustard Sauce

1 Tbsp. hot mustard

2 tsp. water

directions ••

1. Combine ingredients in a small bowl.

CLASSIC RED CHILI

Serves 12

Eating chili is one of your best weight loss allies. It is hearty, healthy, and tasty. The beans, vegetables, and lean meat nourish your body with balanced nutrition. Serve this chili with tortilla chips, grated Monterey Jack cheese, and sour cream.

3 Tbsp. canola oil

1 red bell pepper, diced

1 medium onion, diced

1 lb. lean ground beef

2 (15-oz.) undrained cans diced tomatoes with green chilies or Mexican-style

1 (14-oz.) can tomato sauce

1 (15-oz.) can black beans, rinsed and drained

1 (15-oz.) can kidney beans, rinsed and drained

1 (7-oz.) can fire-roasted green chilies, diced

2 Tbsp. chili powder

2 tsp. ground cumin

½ tsp. cayenne pepper

directions

1. Heat oil in a large skillet over medium heat.

2. Add red pepper and onion and sauté until tender.

3. In a stockpot, brown ground beef on medium heat. Add red pepper and onions.

4. Add remaining ingredients

5. Reduce heat to low and simmer for 15 minutes or until heated through.

BAKED ZITI

People who are trying to lose weight often avoid pasta, especially if they are going low carb. However, I have found that I can lose weight well eating pasta. This recipe is a good choice because it includes ricotta cheese, which is made from whey milk. Whey is one of the best sources of protein you can find.

Serves
12

½ lb. dried ziti pasta, cooked according to package directions

16 oz. ricotta cheese

½ cup shredded Parmesan cheese

½ cup frozen spinach, slightly thawed with water squeezed out

3 cups mozzarella cheese, divided

3 cups prepared premium tomato and basil pasta sauce, divided

¼ cup black olives, sliced

directions •••

1. Preheat oven to 350 degrees.

2. In a large bowl, combine pasta, ricotta cheese, Parmesan cheese, spinach, and half of mozzarella cheese.

3. Grease a 9×13 baking dish. Pour half of pasta sauce on bottom of dish.

4. Add ziti mixture followed by remaining pasta sauce and remaining mozzarella cheese.

5. Sprinkle olives evenly over top. Bake for 20–30 minutes.

ASPARAGUS AND MUSHROOM FRITTATA

Serves 12

Here is a breakfast-type food that is excellent for lunch or dinner. The egg and vegetable combo is excellent for nourishing the body and aiding in the shedding of unwanted weight. Eggs are a super food with vitamins, minerals, and, of course, muscle-building protein.

3 Tbsp. butter

¾ cup chopped onion

2 cloves garlic, minced

½ lb. asparagus, cut into 2-inch pieces (woody end removed)

½ cup sliced button mushrooms

12 eggs, beaten

1 tsp. salt

¼ tsp. black pepper

3 Tbsp. dry bread crumbs

1 cup shredded Monterey Jack cheese

½ cup shredded Parmesan cheese

directions

1. Preheat oven to 350 degrees.

2. In a skillet, heat butter over medium heat. Add onion and garlic. Cook until tender, about 5 minutes.

3. Add asparagus and mushrooms and cook until tender, about 3 minutes.

4. In a medium bowl, combine eggs, salt, and pepper.

5. Fold bread crumbs into onion and asparagus mixture.

6. In a buttered pie or quiche dish, spread asparagus mixture on bottom followed by egg mixture.

7. Sprinkle with cheeses.

8. Bake for 20–25 minutes or until set.

desserts

You may find it surprising to have a dessert section in a diet cookbook, but on an eight-hour diet plan, you can enjoy sweet treats within reason. Of course, it's like your mother always said: "You need to eat your nutritious food before you have treats." As a mother of five trim, healthy kids, I stand by that advice and even hear myself saying it to my kids almost daily.

Rest assured, I have selected these dessert recipes with care and consideration. When you peruse these scrumptious sweets, you might notice that many of the desserts are either fruit or dairy based. This is no accident. I tried to limit flour-based desserts like cakes, cookies, and brownies because of their negative effect on blood sugar. In essence, flour-based desserts tend to raise blood sugar more readily than desserts with eggs, milk, and cream. In moderation, the desserts in this book won't undo your diet. In fact, indulging a sweet tooth every once in a while keeps you from binging, and you are more likely to stick with a diet plan. Enjoy these delightful dishes!

LEMON ICE CREAM

This is simply one of the nicest, freshest flavors of ice cream. Even though I am a chocolate lover, lemon ice cream is my favorite.

Serves
16

3½ cups sugar

¾ cup fresh lemon juice

⅛ cup lemon zest

2 qts. milk

1 pint whipping cream

directions

1. Combine all ingredients in an ice cream maker.

2. Freeze according to manufacturer's directions.

HOMEMADE HOT FUDGE

Serves
10

This is one of the easiest and most delicious frozen desserts that is also sophisticated and looks impressive. Homemade Hot Fudge elevates the taste of quality store-bought ingredients. Enjoy it over your favorite ice cream or frozen yogurt flavor. Add your favorite nut for a little extra taste and nutrition.

½ cup butter

4 Tbsp. unsweetened cocoa

2 cups sugar

1 (14-oz.) can evaporated milk

1 tsp. vanilla extract

pinch of salt

directions ....

1. Melt butter in a medium saucepan. Stir in cocoa and sugar until blended.

2. Add milk, vanilla extract, and salt. Stir to combine.

HONEY ICE CREAM

I won a recipe contest and with it a night's stay at the award-winning Hotel Monaco. In the hotel is the highly rated restaurant Bambara. For dinner we enjoyed steak and roasted chicken. For dessert, we savored their honey ice cream. After that, I had to make it at home.

Serves
8

1½ cups whole milk

1½ cups heavy cream

¼ cup sugar

½ cup local raw honey

pinch of sea salt

5 large egg yolks

directions •

1. Warm the milk, sugar, and salt in a medium saucepan.

2. Pour the cream into a large bowl and add the honey.

3. Whisk the egg yolks in a medium bowl.

4. Slowly pour the milk into the egg yolks, whisking constantly, and then scrape the whole mixture back into the saucepan.

5. Cook over low heat, stirring constantly with a heat-proof spatula, until the mixture is thick enough to coat the spatula.

6. Pour the custard through a strainer and stir it into the cream. Cool over an ice bath. (I filled a large stainless bowl with ice and set a smaller bowl on top.)

7. Chill overnight in the refrigerator.

8. Freeze in an ice cream maker according to the manufacturer's instructions.

APPLE BETTY

Apple Betty recently made it into my list of top ten desserts. It's amazingly good. Simple to be sure, but buttery, sweet, and flavorful. We *love* Apple Betty. Love the name too!

Serves
8

2 cups Fuji apples cored, peeled, and thinly sliced

½ cup sugar

1 tsp. cinnamon

1½ cups crushed graham crackers

½ cup old-fashioned rolled oats

½ cup whole wheat flour

¼ cup brown sugar

½ cup butter, softened

directions •••

1. Preheat oven to 350 degrees.

2. In a medium bowl, mix apples, sugar, and cinnamon and place in a greased 8×8 baking dish.

3. Combine graham crackers, oats, flour, brown sugar, and butter. Crumble mixture over apples.

4. Bake for 30–45 minutes.

5. Serve warm over a scoop of vanilla ice cream.

RASPBERRY PIE

Serves
8

This pie is simply gorgeous and scrumptious. It is a little tart and sweet. Yum!

4 cups frozen raspberries

1 cup granulated sugar

2 tsp. fresh lemon juice

2 Tbsp. flour

1 unbaked pie shell

real, sweetened whipped cream or vanilla ice cream

directions

1. In a saucepan, combine raspberries, sugar, lemon juice, and flour. Simmer for 15 minutes or until thickened.

2. Heat oven to 350 degrees. Cook unfilled pie crust for 10 minutes.

3. Remove pie crust from oven and fill with raspberry pie filling.

4. Bake pie at 350 degrees for 30 minutes.

5. If edges start to brown, cover edges with strips of aluminum foil.

6. Let pie set in refrigerator for 3 hours before serving with whipped cream or vanilla ice cream.

LAVENDER SHORTBREAD COOKIE ICE CREAM SANDWICHES

Serves 12

My daughter and I went to a gourmet ice cream stand called Esmeralda on the corner of Notre-Dame Cathedral in Paris. (Don't you love the name Esmeralda, borrowed from Victor Hugo's epic novel *The Hunchback of Notre Dame*?) They serve up the most unusual ice cream flavors, including basil, lavender, and tiramisu. This recipe is decadent. For a fun little touch, I filled two lavender shortbread cookies with homemade honey ice cream. The cookies are flaky, and the ice cream tastes like crème brûlée.

1½ cups butter, softened

2/3 cup granulated sugar

¼ cup powdered sugar

1 Tbsp. dried lavender

1 tsp. fresh lemon zest

2½ cups flour

½ cup cornstarch

¼ tsp. salt

Honey Ice Cream (p. 117)

directions

1. In a medium bowl, cream together the butter and sugars until light and fluffy.

2. Mix in lavender and lemon zest.

3. In a separate bowl, combine flour, cornstarch, and salt.

4. Mix flour mixture into butter mixture until well blended.

5. Divide dough into two balls, wrap in plastic wrap, and flatten to about 1 inch thick. Refrigerate until firm, about 1 hour.

6. Preheat oven to 325 degrees.

7. On a lightly floured surface, roll the dough out to ¼-inch thickness.

8. Cut dough into shapes with cookie cutters.

9. Place dough shapes on a cookie sheet and bake for 18–20 minutes or until cookies begin to brown at the edges.

10. Cool for a few minutes on baking sheets, then transfer to wire racks to cool completely.

11. Add a scoop of Honey Ice Cream between two cooled cookies and gently press. Cover in plastic wrap and freeze until ready to serve.

VANILLA FROZEN YOGURT

Serves
6

I started my search for homemade frozen yogurt recipes after I became obsessed with Red Mango's frozen yogurt! The ingredients are simple, but the outcome is delicious!

3 cups Greek yogurt

$^2/_3$ **cup sugar**

1 tsp. real vanilla extract

directions ....

1. Combine all ingredients and refrigerate for one hour.

2. Place mixture in ice cream maker and freeze according to manufacturer's directions. (You will need ice and rock salt.)

CHOCOLATE RASPBERRY TRUFFLES

A few years ago, I took this dessert to a potluck dinner. One of the men there raved about how good they were. So I took him a small plate for him to enjoy. He was an artist and drew me a picture of them with colored pencils as a thank you note. I love that drawing as much as I do this chocolate confection.

Serves
12

1 (15-oz.) can sweetened condensed milk

2 Tbsp. butter

2 Tbsp. seedless raspberry jam

1 Tbsp. raspberry extract

2 (12-oz.) bags Ghirardelli semisweet chocolate chips

½ cup confectioners' sugar

directions ••

1. In a microwave safe bowl, heat milk, butter, jam, and extract for 3 minutes on high heat.

2. Pour in chocolate chips and stir until completely melted. Cover with plastic wrap and freeze for 30 minutes.

3. Form balls using a teaspoon and roll in confectioners' sugar.

4. Let set in refrigerator until ready to serve.

MUD PIES

Mud Pies are one of those fancy but simple desserts. Using individual-sized ice cream cartons gives you portion control and a pretty presentation.

Serves
6

1 sleeve graham crackers, crushed

¼ cup butter, melted

6 (4-oz.) cartons Häagen-Dazs chocolate ice cream

1½ cups Homemade Hot Fudge (p. 116)

sweetened whipped cream

directions

1. Combine graham crackers with butter.

2. Using a fork, press 1½ tablespoons of graham cracker mixture on top of ice cream in each carton.

3. Peel paper carton from ice cream and invert onto individual dessert plates.

4. Pour 2 tablespoons of warmed hot fudge over ice cream.

5. Top with a dollop of whipped cream.

6. Serve immediately.

CHARLOTTE'S CARROT CAKE

Serves
8

This cake is decidedly better the second day, because the flavors develop and the frosting thickens. This is my Grandmother's classic carrot cake recipe. You can try it as mini bundt cakes or even cupcakes. Go ahead and add copious amounts of Cream Cheese Frosting on top.

1 cup oil

2 cups sugar

3 eggs, beaten

2 cups peeled and shredded carrots

1 (6-oz.) can crushed pineapple, drained

3 cups flour

1 tsp. salt

1 tsp. baking soda

1 tsp. cinnamon

2 tsp. vanilla

1 cup crushed walnuts

1 cup raisins

Cream Cheese Frosting
    (recipe follows)

directions

1. Preheat oven to 350 degrees.

2. Mix oil and sugar together in a large bowl.

3. Add eggs, carrots, and pineapple.

4. In a separate bowl, mix flour, salt, baking soda, and cinnamon.

5. Add dry ingredients mixture to sugar mixture.

6. Add vanilla, walnuts, and raisins. Stir until combined.

7. Bake in a greased 9×13 baking dish for 40–45 minutes or until a toothpick comes out clean. (If baking mini bundts or cupcakes, decrease time to 20–25 minutes.)

8. Spread Cream Cheese Frosting over cooled cake.

9. Refrigerate until ready to serve.

Cream Cheese Frosting

3 cups powdered sugar

¼ cup butter, softened

4 oz. cream cheese, softened

1 tsp. vanilla

directions

1. Mix all ingredients in a medium bowl until smooth.

CRÈME BRÛLÉE

Serves
10

This dessert is a little tricky and does take some careful attention, but if you love crème brûlée, the effort will be worth it! Crème Brûlée is an elegant little custard that does not spike blood sugar like other desserts.

10 large egg yolks

1 cup granulated sugar, plus extra to caramelize top

4 cups heavy whipping cream

2 Tbsp. pure vanilla extract

directions •

1. Using a wire whisk or electric mixer, vigorously whisk egg yolks with granulated sugar in a large bowl until mixture becomes light in color and sugar has dissolved a bit. Set aside.

2. In a medium-sized saucepan, combine heavy cream with vanilla. Bring the mixture to a simmer. When small bubbles have formed around the edges of the cream, it is ready.

3. Gradually pour the cream mixture into the egg and sugar mixture. Gently mix by hand. Chill and cover mixture with plastic wrap pierced several times to release steam. Chill overnight.

4. Preheat oven to 350 degrees. Place individual ramekins in a baking pan large enough to hold 8–10 six-ounce custard cups and deep enough to allow for the water to be added (reaching at least halfway up the sides of the ramekins).

5. Fill ramekins ¾ full of mixture. Place pan in preheated oven and pour hot water into baking pan so the water level reaches halfway up the sides of the ramekins.

Cover pan with a sheet of heavy-duty aluminum foil, sealing the edges to retain steam. Cook for 40–50 minutes or until custards are set. To determine if done, gently shake the individual ramekins; if center is still liquid-like or wobbly, return custards to oven and continue to cook, checking every 5–7 minutes, until it has just set with a small area in the center (the size of a quarter) still a bit loose.

6. Remove ramekins from baking pan and chill custard in refrigerator for several hours.

7. To serve, put a thin layer of granulated sugar atop each custard. Using a blow torch over a heat- and flame-proof surface (like a large cookie sheet or baking sheet), caramelize sugar, working from the outside in toward the the middle and keeping the torch in constant motion. Sugar should be golden brown and caramelized, never black. If burnt, let the sugar layer cool a few minutes and then peel it away with a paring knife and begin again. (Alternately, you could caramelize the sugar under a broiler, keeping a careful watch over it and rotating it to cook evenly. This takes about 2 minutes.)

POACHED PEARS
WITH CINNAMON HONEY SYRUP

Serves
4

This is not only a healthy and tasty treat, but it is also an elegant and pretty dessert.

3 cups pear or apple juice

¾ cups sugar

1 cup water

2 Tbsp. honey

1 tsp. cinnamon

1 tsp. fresh lemon juice

4 firm ripe pears, peeled with stems intact

vanilla ice cream

directions ....

1. In a saucepan large enough to hold all the pears, combine the juice, sugar water, honey, cinnamon, and lemon juice.

2. Bring the mixture to a simmer, stirring occasionally, until the honey has melted. Add the pears and simmer for 25–30 minutes, turning occasionally, until the pears are tender but not falling apart.

3. Remove the pears from the liquid and allow to cool.

4. Continue to simmer the liquid until it thickens and is reduced by half, 15–20 minutes. Cool to room temperature.

5. Place each pear on a small serving plate with a scoop of vanilla ice cream. Drizzle with the cinnamon honey syrup. Serve immediately.

VANILLA CUSTARD WITH FRESH FRUIT

Creamy custard is simply delicious, especially when accompanied by fresh fruit in season.

½ cup sugar

3 Tbsp. cornstarch

½ tsp. salt

4 eggs yolks

3 cups milk

2 Tbsp. butter

2 tsp. vanilla

fresh fruit of choice; like cut mangoes, blackberries, and raspberries

directions

1. Bring sugar, cornstarch, salt, egg yolks, and milk to a boil in a heavy saucepan.

2. Whisking constantly, boil mixture for 20 minutes or until thick. Remove from heat. Stir in butter and vanilla

3. Divide into 8 dessert cups and chill for 2 hours, covered, in the refrigerator.

4. Serve with fresh fruit.

PEANUT BUTTER COOKIES

Serves 24

The taste and texture of these cookies makes them absolutely the best peanut butter cookies I've ever had. Serve with a big glass of cold milk! If you want to add a little chocolate, break off squares of a Hershey's chocolate bar and place in the middle of each cookie as soon as they are out of the oven. Even though these cookies have white flour, the peanut butter makes them a nice treat even when you're trying to lose weight—just don't eat the whole dozen.

½ cup creamy peanut butter

½ cup butter

½ cup white sugar, plus more

½ cup brown sugar

1 egg

1¼ cup flour

¼ tsp. salt

¾ tsp. baking soda

½ tsp. baking powder

directions

1. In a medium bowl, cream together peanut butter, butter, and sugars. Add egg and stir to combine.

2. In a small bowl, combine flour, salt, baking soda, and baking powder.

3. Combine flour mixture with butter mixture. Refrigerate for 3 hours or overnight.

4. Make 1¼-inch balls. Roll balls in white sugar. Place on a non-greased cookie sheet 2 inches apart and flatten with a fork in a crisscross pattern.

5. Bake in a 350-degree oven for 12–14 minutes or until tops are golden brown.

BERRY BANANA SHERBET

Sherbet dessert is low fat, refreshing, and a snap to make. It is fantastic for brunches and last-minute desserts. Try serving it with vanilla Pirouette rolled wafers.

2 bananas, sliced

1 cup blueberries

2 cups raspberries

½ gallon pineapple sherbet

directions ....

1. In a large bowl, fold bananas, blueberries, and raspberries into pineapple sherbet.

2. Put in an airtight container until ready to serve.

BROILED GRAPEFRUIT

When trying to lose weight, grapefruit may be one of your best helps. This is a juicy, easy, and nutritious dessert you could eat every day and drop pounds while you're at it.

Serves
4

2 grapefruit, cut in half

½ Tbsp. sugar

2 tsp. ground cinnamon

directions

1. Place grapefruit, facing up, on a small cookie sheet.

2. Sprinkle grapefruit evenly with sugar and cinnamon.

3. Broil for 3–5 minutes or until sugar and cinnamon mixture is melted and slightly caramelized.

TROPICAL ICE POPS

Serves
12

Fruit ice pops are not just for kids. You can't go wrong eating frozen pops loaded with healthy tropical fruits. Scrumptious on a stick.

4 cups watermelon chunks

2 kiwis, peeled and cut into small chunks

½ cup mango cut into small chunks

directions ••

1. Puree watermelon, kiwi, and mango in a blender until smooth.

2. Pour mixture into ice pop molds and freeze until set, about 2 hours.

STRAWBERRY COCONUT ICE CREAM

This ice cream has a unique tropical flavor since it calls for coconut milk rather than regular milk and cream. It's a fun frozen treat and family favorite.

Serves **10**

1 (13.5-oz.) can sweetened coconut milk

2 cups cream

½ cup sugar

2 tsp. vanilla

2 firm bananas, sliced

½ cup crushed pineapple

1½ cups sweetened, frozen strawberries

directions

1. Put all ingredients in an ice cream maker and freeze according to manufacturer's directions.

LEMON MOUSSE

Serves 8

After I sampled this at a lady's luncheon, I figured out how to make it so I could share this lite, delicious, and delightful mini dessert with my family.

1 cup whipping cream

1 Tbsp. powdered sugar

5 oz. lemon curd (found by jams and jellies at supermarket)

16 small phyllo shells

berries for garnish

directions

1. In a medium bowl, combine cream and sugar and beat until stiff.

2. Add warmed lemon curd. Beat until smooth and combined.

3. Fill each phyllo shell with 1 tablespoon custard and top with 3 berries of choice.

CHOCOLATE-COVERED STRAWBERRIES

Who doesn't love chocolate-covered strawberries? They are easy to make, calling for a mere two ingredients. They are also a romantic food.

Serves
6

½ cup milk chocolate chips

6 large strawberries

¼ cup white chocolate chips

directions •

1. Melt milk chocolate chips in the microwave at 20-second intervals, stirring between until melted.

2. Dip clean, dry strawberries in milk chocolate and then place on a cookie sheet or a plate lined with waxed paper.

3. Let sit in refrigerator until set (about 5 minutes).

4. Melt white chocolate chips in microwave at 20-second intervals, stirring between until melted.

5. Using a spoon, drizzle white chocolate across chocolate-covered strawberries.

6. Return to plate and let sit in refrigerator for another 5 minutes or until chocolate is set.

Notes: Do not get water in chocolate. It will harden or seize. Do not burn chocolate. It is unforgiving, and you will have to start over.

SHAUNA EVANS

ROASTED CINNAMON ALMONDS

Serves 8

At Christmastime in Germany, street vendors sell fresh roasted cinnamon almonds. The cinnamon scents the air with a wonderful holiday aroma.

2 cups whole almonds

½ cup sugar

1 tsp. cinnamon

½ tsp. salt

2 Tbsp. butter

1 tsp. vanilla extract

directions

1. In a skillet, combine almonds, sugar, cinnamon, salt, and butter and cook over medium heat, stirring constantly until sugar melts and turns brown.

2. Remove from heat and stir in vanilla.

3. Spread onto a buttered baking sheet and cool.

COCOA SNAP ICE CREAM SANDWICHES

A few years ago, I made these frozen treats for a women's group. They devoured them like kids at an ice cream truck.

Serves
12

½ cup flour

½ cup sugar

¼ cup unsweetened cocoa powder

½ tsp. baking powder

¼ tsp. salt

2 Tbsp. butter, softened

1 large egg, beaten lightly

ice cream of choice

directions ••

1. In a bowl, whisk flour, sugar, cocoa powder, baking powder, and salt with fingers. Blend in butter. Stir in egg until combined. Cover dough and chill until firm, about 1 hour.

2. Preheat oven to 400 degrees. Spoon tablespoonfuls of dough onto a greased cookie sheet. Press flat with spatula or fingers. Cook for 8–9 minutes or until cocoa snaps are set but not hard. Cool cocoa snaps on a rack. (They will become crisp as they cool.)

3. Fill two cocoa snaps with your favorite ice cream flavor. If not eating right away, wrap each ice cream sandwich in plastic and freeze.

OATMEAL, CHOCOLATE, AND WALNUT COOKIES

Serves 24

I have been a cookie connoisseur since junior high school. These cookies are absolutely addicting and a good cookie choice with the oats and walnuts.

1 cup butter, softened

¾ cup brown sugar

¾ cup granulated sugar

2 eggs

1 tsp. vanilla

½ tsp. cinnamon

1½ cups flour

1 tsp. baking soda

½ tsp. salt

3 cups old-fashioned rolled oats

2 cups semisweet chocolate chips

½ cup crushed walnuts (optional)

directions

1. Preheat oven to 350 degrees.

2. In a large bowl, cream butter and sugars together. Add eggs and stir to combine. Add vanilla and cinnamon.

3. In a separate bowl, combine flour, baking soda, and salt.

4. Add flour mixture to butter mixture and stir. Add oats, chocolate chips, and optional walnuts. Stir to combine.

5. Using a tablespoon, form dough balls and place on a greased cookie sheet or baking stone.

6. Bake for 11–12 minutes or until golden brown.

BERRY PEACH COBBLER

Serves
16

Overall, cobblers are a better dessert choice for weight loss than pie because there is usually more fruit and less crust.

2 cups fresh peach slices

2 cups fresh raspberries
or blackberries

2 tsp. fresh-squeezed
lemon juice

⅓ cup + 1½ Tbsp. sugar, divided

2 Tbsp. + ¾ cup flour, divided

¼ tsp. salt

1½ tsp. baking powder

2 Tbsp. butter, chilled
and cut into small pieces

½ cup heavy cream

premium vanilla ice cream

directions

1. Preheat oven to 400 degrees.

2. Place peaches, berries, and lemon juice in a small bowl.

3 Toss with ⅓ cup sugar and 2 tablespoons flour. Set aside.

4. In a bowl, mix ¾ cup flour, salt, baking powder, 1 tablespoon sugar, and butter until mixture resembles small peas.

5. Slowly add cream and mix until dough comes together.

6. Fill a greased 2-quart baking dish with berry mixture.

7. Drop dough in clumps over berry mixture.

8. Sprinkle with remaining ½ tablespoon sugar.

9. Bake for 20 minutes or until bubbly and golden brown.

10. Serve with vanilla ice cream.

FROZEN YOGURT POPS

Serves 8

These tasty frozen yogurt treats do not require an ice cream maker. They are quick and easy, kids and adults love them, and they are good for you.

2 (8-oz.) pkgs. fruit yogurt
(strawberry, raspberry,
mango, peach)

1 cup whipped cream, softened

1 (8-oz.) pkg. sweetened frozen fruit

directions

1. Combine all ingredients in a medium bowl.

2. Carefully pour mixture into 8 popsicle molds and freeze until set, at least 2 hours.

STRAWBERRY SOUP

Are you looking for a summer soup? Then try this chilled fruit soup. Pair it with a sandwich or salad for a lovely lunch.

1 lb. fresh strawberries, stems removed

1 cup whipping cream

6 oz. lemon-lime soda pop

1 Tbsp. granulated sugar

directions

1. Place all ingredients in a blender and pulse until smooth.

2. Serve in 8-ounce dessert cups. Garnish with fresh mint leaves and fanned strawberries.

CHOCOLATE-COVERED FROZEN BANANAS

Serves
4

Ever since I was a teenager, I have associated chocolate-covered frozen bananas with amusement parks because that is where I first sunk my teeth into one and fell in love with it. It is always nice when I can make a vendor-type treat at home.

4 bananas

sucker sticks

1 cup milk chocolate chips

toppings of choice (chopped peanuts, shredded sweetened coconut, etc.)

directions

1. Peel bananas and put a sucker stick in each, leaving 2 inches.

2. Wrap bananas individually in plastic wrap and freeze for at least 2 hours.

3. Melt chocolate chips in microwave for 20-second intervals, stirring between each interval until melted.

4. Dip frozen bananas in melted chocolate to cover.

5. With bananas on a wax paper–lined plate, sprinkle nuts, coconut, or other topping of choice over bananas before chocolate sets.

RICE PUDDING

Rice pudding is a wonderful comfort food. It is creamy and slightly sweet with a hint of spices. It's a snap to make and a great way to utilize leftover cooked rice.

1½ cup cooked short-grain rice

2 cups whole milk, divided

⅓ cup sugar

¼ tsp. salt

1 large egg

1 tsp. vanilla extract

⅔ cup raisins

1 tsp. cinnamon

directions

1. In a medium saucepan, combine rice, 1½ cups milk, sugar, and salt.

2. Cook over medium heat until mixture thickens, about 15 minutes.

3. In a bowl, stir egg, vanilla, and ½ cup milk together. Add to saucepan.

4. Add raisins and cinnamon and stir.

5. Cook for 2 more minutes.

Flavored and Vitamin Waters ≪≪≪≪≪≪≪≪≪≪

Flavored and vitamin waters are very popular among Americans. However, where some flavored waters have merit, many of them are subpar, loaded with sugar and extra calories that you don't need or want. Even some of the vitamin waters have been proven to hurt the enamel on teeth. So read the label and choose natural-flavored waters without sugar or, better yet, make your own.

In January 2013, my family and I traveled to Newport Beach, California, and we stayed at the Marriott Hotel. In the hotel's lobby were two large drink dispensers full of interesting natural-flavored waters for guests. One day, honeydew melons and watermelon slices would be bobbing in the water. The next day, oranges and grapefruit were floating lazily. Each morning, I would bound down to the lobby to see what other beautiful water concoctions they created for my refreshment and benefit.

Homemade flavored waters are ideal because you are using fresh and natural ingredients at a fraction of the cost of store-purchased waters. These vitamin waters are not only tasty but also healthy. They are much like soup in that the fruit and vegetables leach out their vitamins and minerals into the water. So when you taste the strawberry or cucumber flavor, you are experiencing the antioxidant power of the food. Pretty cool!

Flavored Water Variations

In a large pitcher of ice water, add any of the following:

1. Honeydew melon and watermelon slices with rinds intact

2. Grapefruit and orange slices

3. Fresh strawberries

4. Fresh lemon and lime slices

5. Fresh cranberries and lime slices (lovely for the holidays)

6. Cucumber slices, lime slices, and fresh mint leaves (for a cleansing water)

Index

INDEX

>>> About the Author

Shauna Schmidt Evans was born and raised in northern Utah beneath the Wasatch Mountains. She was a competitive athlete. Her high school cheer squad was ninth in the nation, and she took fourth place in her age category when she ran her first St. George marathon at the age of eighteen. She has completed three half marathons and three full marathons.

Shauna graduated from Brigham Young University with a bachelor of science in nursing. At BYU, she taught in the anatomy lab. She married Joe Evans, BYU backup quarterback to Ty Detmer, in 1992. They have five fit, athletic children. Shauna is a water aerobics instructor and continues her nursing education in subjects regarding nutrition, exercise, and overall good health. Health and fitness have always been of special interest to her.

Shauna is the author of *What Goes with What for Baby Rooms: Decorating Made Easy* and *Sweet and Savory: Award-Winning Recipes Made Easy*. She has won over ten recipe contests; has appeared on *The Daily Dish*, *Good Things Utah*, *Studio 5*, and *Fox 13 News*; and has taught at the Salt Lake Home Show.

ALSO BY SHAUNA EVANS

*W*hether you're looking for a savory barbecue sauce for your next backyard get-together or a show-stopping dessert, you've come to the right kitchen to find it.

Discover top-secret family recipes like Evans Family Award-Winning Fudge and German Plum Streusel! You will never be at a loss for great-tasting meals when you have these easy award-winning recipes at your side!